Eucharistic Bread-Baking As Ministry

Tony Begonja

Resource Publications, Inc.
San Jose, California

Editorial director: *Kenneth Guentert*
Managing editor: *Kathi Drolet*
Copy editor: *Alice Hugh Brown*
Art director: *Terri Ysseldyke-All*
Step-by-step photos: *Tony Begonja*
Wedding photos: *Dick and Sue Hunter*

Library of Congress Cataloging in Publication Data
Begonja, Tony, 1958-
    Eucharistic bread-baking as ministry / Tony Begonja.
      p. cm.
    ISBN 0-89390-200-4 : $7.95
    1. Bread. 2.Bread—religious aspects. I. Title.
TX769.B334 1991   91-4084
641.5'66--dc20

5 4 3 2 1 95 94 93 92 91

Contents

Acknowledgements

The Wheat-and-Honey Recipe in this book is my adaptation of a Trappist recipe and is similar to the Franciscan Mass Bread recipe that has been around for years.

The Wheat-Only Recipe given is my adaptation of one created by Deacon Bill Mallory (a professional baker) of Hailey, Idaho and distributed by the FDLC at its 1981 meeting in Idaho. Thank you, Bill!

The "Gaelen's Bread" Recipe is from Gaelen Evans of Mission Hills, Kansas. Thank you, Gaelen!

The Greek/Eastern Rites Recipe is from Father Theoharis Theoharis of Overland Park, Kansas. Thank you, Father Theoharis!

The St. Gregory's Abbey Altar Bread Recipe is from Father Robert Hutcherson of Raytown, Missouri. Thank you Fr. Hutcherson!

I am grateful to Dick and Sue Hunter for taking all those beautiful wedding pictures and in particular this one (see cover) of Father Lou Leyh, Fran and myself.

To the memory
of our good friend,
Lou Leyh (1928-1987),
who went home to the Lord
a few months after he presided
at our wedding Mass.

Introduction

About the Recipes

This book is intended for use by any Christian
parishes and congregations who care deeply about
how they celebrate the Eucharist. In that vein, six
diverse recipes have been included, as well as
citations of pertinent rubrics from some of the major
Christian confessions. If you are in doubt as to which
recipes are allowed for use in your situation, please
consult the appropriate pastoral authority (your
pastor, liturgy/worship office, or bishop).

Scripture and the Eucharist

Let's look at some passages from Scripture about
the Eucharist:

I myself am the bread of life. (Jn 6:35, NAB)

'Whoever feeds on my flesh and drinks my blood has life
eternal and I will raise him up on the last day. For my flesh
is real food, and my blood is real drink. The one who feeds
on my flesh and drinks my blood remains in me and I in
him.' (Jn 6:54-56, NAB)

As they were eating, Jesus took a small loaf of bread and
blessed it and broke it apart and gave it to the disciples and

said, 'Take it and eat it, for this is my body.' And he took a cup of wine and gave thanks for it and gave it to them and said, 'Each one drink from it, for this is my blood, sealing the New Covenant. It is poured out to forgive the sins of multitudes.' (Mt 26:26-28, TLB)

'...do this as a rememberance of me.' (Lk 22:19c, NAB)

Then they recounted what had happened on the road and how they had come to know him in the breaking of bread. (Lk 24:35, NAB)

[The 3,000] joined with the other believers in regular attendance at the apostles teaching sessions and at the Communion services and prayer meetings. A deep sense of awe was on them all, and the apostles did many miracles. And all the believers met together constantly and shared everything with each other, selling their possessions and dividing with those in need. They worshiped together regularly in the Temple each day, met in small groups in homes for Communion, and shared their meals with great joy and thankfulness, praising God. The whole city was favorable to them, and each day God added to them all who were being saved. (Acts 2:42-46, TLB)

On the first day of the week when we gathered for the breaking of bread,... (Acts 20:7, NAB)

The Lord's command to his people is quite clear: we Christians need to assemble regularly in order to worship the Lord, hear the Scriptures and celebrate the breaking of the bread (the Eucharist). When we celebrate the breaking of the bread, we need to do it with richness and care because it is God's banquet for us. The eating and drinking in this celebration are important and not simply token. There is a need for good bread to be consecrated, broken and eaten; and a need for good wine to be blessed and drunk.

This is where bread bakers have an important role to play. Our task is to bake the bread used in celebrations of the Eucharist. This duty, like participating in the Eucharist itself, is not reserved for priests, ministers and religious, but can be done by you and me — ordinary Christians. Baking altar bread is a **ministry**, and like all ministries, it can't be done without prayer, love and attention to detail. The purpose of this book is to help you not only to properly perform this ministry of baking altar breads, but also understand what it's all about.

Chapter 1

Altar Breads: Past and Present

Early Jewish-Christian Practice

I. The Last Supper

According to Joseph Stallings (in his marvelous book, *Rediscovering Passover: A Complete Guide for Christians*), the Last Supper that Jesus, his rabbinical school and their families and friends celebrated was most certainly a Passover seder. As such, the bread used was baked according to a precise custom:

> Only pure water and pure flour could be used in the making of the [Passover] matzot. Matzah could be made from either wheat or barley flour. In the first century, however, barley flour was preferred because Passover was associated with the barley harvest that occurred at that time and also because the Hebrew name for spring, *aviv*, was taken from the word for "new ears of barley," or *abib*.

The ritual matzah was typically baked by a team of three women. One poured water into flour in a mixing bowl. Another kneaded it. The third

shaped the dough into round, flat loaves and placed these
into the oven [an oven dedicated to the task of baking the
Passover matzot] to quickly bake....The matzot of the first
century were not like the thin, flat, crisp machine-made
ones that we are familiar with today. They were thicker,
softer and chewier. [The bakers] frequently cut designs into
them with special tools.[1]

The Passover meal involved, among other
things, the use of at least three loaves of matzah, and
each loaf had a name: Kohen (priest), Levy (Levite)
and Yisrael (People of God).[2] The ritual for the
Passover meal was elaborate and had many parts.
One involved a children's game where the players
would take the afikoman (pieces of lamb set aside for
dessert), hide it and "extort" their elders for
"ransom."[3]

The loaf called Levy was also known as the
"bread of poverty." "Jesus explained this bread, not
in the traditional words, 'This is the bread of poverty
which our forefathers ate in the land of Egypt' but in
the then unheard-of words, 'This is My body.'"[4] This
happened during the Ha Motzi (the Blessing of
Bread) during the Passover meal. Jesus identified
himself with the paschal lamb. By instructing his
disciples 'This matzah is me.' Jesus clearly meant, "I
am your real Passover sacrifice."[5]

II. The Still-Jewish Early Christians.

Not only had Jesus organized his followers as a
rabbinical school, Beyt Y'shu'a, but also as a
chavurah, a Passover society — a fellowship of Jews
who traveled to Jerusalem together each year for the
Passover. "At the Last Supper, Jesus elevated his

chavurah to a covenant fellowship (chavurah ha-chesed)." As such, the early church began to think of itself as a "family bound together by the flesh and blood of Jesus" and was often organized much like a Jewish extended family. This "family" shared table fellowship frequently — especially the Sabbath meal and the Havdalah-Agape each week and the Passover each year.[6]

The Sabbath Meal. During the sabbath meal shared each Friday evening, the early believers blessed and shared two loaves of bread. These loaves, now called challah, were made with flour, eggs, sugar (or honey), a leavening agent (now yeast), and salt. For the liquid and shortening, water and vegetable oil were used instead of milk and butter, so that this bread could be eaten at a meat meal. "Archaeological evidence suggests that the sabbath challah of the first century was made into round loaves with deep crosses cut into the top. The Christian mother cut I and X into loaves which represented Iesous Xristos (Jesus Christ)." This was an evolution from what was done before, when "a simple X" was cut into the loaves. This represented "the ancient form of the last letter of the Hebrew alphabet, 'taw', meaning 'good' and the 'sign of the Lord'."[7]

At the sabbath meal, "while the wine was blessed and shared and the Kiddush was recited, the two sabbath loaves were covered with a special embroidered cloth." After the Kiddush, the father of the family or extended family uncovered the challah and recited a short blessing. He then tore or cut apart one loaf into portions and shared the sabbath bread with everyone at table. "The sharing of the kiddush cup and sabbath loaf represented the unity of the whole family."[8]

The Havdalah-Agape. Pious Jews of the first century often ate a ritual supper on Saturday evening — at the close of the Sabbath. The early Christians took this first-day-of-the-week supper and made it their own since Jesus, their beloved teacher and Messiah, rose from the dead on the morning of that day of the week. (Note here that the Hebrew "day" began at sunset, not midnight.) "This supper became the primary supper of the Christian community."[9]

During this meal, like the Passover, three loaves of bread were blessed. This was done because the Havdalah-Agape was also an *anamnesis-zikkaron*, re-actualization, of the Last Supper. "These loaves were a reminder of the three sheets of the watched matzot that Jesus blessed at the Last Supper and of the three persons in the Holy Trinity. Two of these loaves were broken and shared as the hamotzi of the agape-supper. The third loaf was set aside with the Cup of Blessings for the Eucharist at the conclusion of their supper." At the end of the meal, a lengthy grace (thanksgiving) was said and then those assembled "shared the body and blood of Jesus."[10] It is not clear what kind of bread (matzah or challah) was used for the Havdalah-Agape.

The Passover. The early Christians continued to celebrate the Passover each year.

"As long as the Jerusalem community was the official church, the Christian observance of Passover was identical with the Jewish. The ceremony was

exactly the same, but for the Christians, Christ
became the central focus of the ritual. The seder
became a reliving of the Last Supper, death, burial
and resurrection of Jesus. Every movement and
comment Jesus made on the evening of the Last
Supper was re- enacted and repeated.... This
reactualization of the Last Supper in each succeeding
Passover seder influenced the observance of the
weekly Eucharist so much that [eventually] the
weekly Eucharist of the Havdalah-Agape became a
miniature seder."[11]

In the post-temple Christian Passover, the three
obligatory loaves of matzot were renamed from Kohen,
Levy and Yisrael to Father, Son and Holy Spirit.
"Christians took the Son (the middle loaf), broke it,
wrapped it in a white cloth to represent a shroud and
'buried' it in a hiding place to be brought back for the
afikoman — as a dramatization of Jesus' death, burial
and resurrection.... The larger half of the middle loaf
was used at the end of the meal-liturgy for the afikoman
("the last thing eaten"); this was blessed and shared as
Holy Communion. Following the Passover regulations,
each one "received a piece of the Lamb of God [at least]
'the size of an olive'."

Note here that in the post-temple (i.e., after the
destruction of the temple) passovers, both the
Christian and Pharisaic Jews transferred much
symbolism from the lamb to the matzah. The
Christians continued to serve lamb as the main
course of the meal. "The two symbols [of lamb and
bread] flowed gently together in Christ." The

Pharisees phased out the use of lamb (except for a token bone) entirely.[12]

Also, "when it was time in the meal to explain the meaning of the paschal lamb, unleavened bread and bitter herb, the Christian paterfamilias told how each one of these also represented Christ: Jesus is the Lamb of God (Jn 1:29); Jesus is the True Bread that came down from Heaven (Jn 6:32-58); Jesus died on the cross in a single perfect sacrifice that atoned for all of our sins (Heb 10:10-18)."[13]

According to Stallings, the Jewish Christians continued to celebrate the Eucharist weekly and annually, in this manner, for quite some time.

III. The Practice of the Gentile Church

Leavened Bread. For a long time there was "no great importance" placed on the distinction between leavened and unleavened bread.[14] In fact, most of the Gentile Christian writings and art suggest that the church, both east and west, typically employed regular loaves of leavened bread for the Eucharist. Four images come to mind:

"Addressing the newly baptized, Athanasius of Alexandria said: 'You will see the deacons bringing the loaves and the chalice and placing them on the altar'."[15]

"The pope then washed his hands and went to the altar where the communion loaves and chalice were waiting.... Then [he] broke off the first piece of bread and communion was distributed.... Communion was received standing, the bread being placed in the hand and the wine being sipped through a small tube...."[16]

A mosaic in the present day Church of San Vitale in Ravenna, Italy, which used to serve as a royal chapel for the Christian emperors of Rome, "depicts the Emperor Justinian holding the large, leavened loaf of bread that will become the Eucharist."[17]

An early ritual book, *Ordo I*, describes a significant fraction rite: "Bishops and priests break all the consecrated loaves, which acolytes carry in linen sacks to these various celebrants and their places…[this rite] took some time when the congregation was a large one. "

Another early ritual book, the Gregorian sacramentary, refers to "the loaves piled upon the altar (*muneribus altaria cumulata*)."[18]

Lay Involvement. All this bread was baked by parishioners, who found great spiritual benefit in doing so. Again, some examples:

St. Augustine wrote that "his mother let no day pass without bringing her offering [her bread] to the altar."[19]

Hippolytus wrote, "Those to be baptized will bring nothing with them except what each one brings for the Eucharist. For it is fitting that those who become worthy of doing so should provide the gifts on that same occasion. "[20]

About C.E. 458 Victor of Vita, in North Africa, wrote that "a blind man who had been miraculously cured approached the altar in order to present 'the offering which the bishop receives for his salvation'."[21]

A widow of Lyons "believed firmly that her deceased husband 'found rest on the day when she presented the offering [of bread] to the Lord for his soul'."[22]

Not only was the bread to be brought by the faithful, but in some churches *all* the faithful were

expected to bring some. Any that was not used for
the Eucharist was used either by the pastors or given
to the poor.[23] Saint Cyprian, for instance, criticized a
"matron who dared come with empty hands: 'You
are rich and well to do; yet you think you celebrate
the Lord's Supper even though you... come to it
without an offering and receive part of the offering
brought by a poor person. Consider the widow in the
gospel...'." There were times, though, when bringing
the offering of bread didn't "work" for some. For
example, "St. Gregory tells of a woman who when
receiving holy communion recognized a piece of the
bread she had baked herself and, because her faith
was unenlightened, had trouble accepting it was the
Body of Christ...."[24]

Shape of the Bread. Most of the ancient writers
reported that people just brought whatever they used
at home. However, in some places it was the custom
"to present loaves shaped in the form of a cross,"
which apparently facilitated the fraction. In addition,
"some ancient iron molds have been found which
bear an inscription or the monogram of Christ."[25]

Unleavened Bread Appears. The consistent use
of unleavened bread for the Eucharist, and a
seemingly corresponding contempt toward the use of
leavened altar bread, first occurred among the
Armenians. During the reign of Emperor Maurice
(C.E. 582-602), Catholicos Moses II refused to journey
to Constantinople, saying: "God grant...that I may
never eat baked bread...."[26]

A Decline in Involvement. As time went on,
though, with fewer and fewer Christians who were both

instructed well and personally "converted," fewer came to the Lord's table to receive holy communion. Around C.E. 390, John Chrysostom of Antioch lamented, "It is in vain that we ascend to the altar; there is no one to participate.[27] So even though loaves of leavened bread were still being consecrated, most of it was not eaten, at least by lay people. In addition, in the eastern churches, at some point the responsibility for baking/bringing the bread was taken from the people and given to the clergy, who were supposed to bake "to the accompaniment of suitable prayers."[28]

IV. The Middle Ages.

The French Influence. By the ninth century, most Christians did not regularly receive holy communion, even though they were present at liturgy. In addition to a possible lack of teaching and personal conversion, certain strange notions, sensibilities and practices began to spread into the rest of the church from France. Among these were:

> Discouraging lay people from receiving holy communion "lest it bring damnation rather than salvation upon their souls. "[29]

> Lay people were not to touch the sacred elements with their hands. Instead they were to be fed the blessed bread and wine by the priest, the bread being placed on the tongue.[30] In addition they were to receive communion kneeling rather than standing. This was apparently intended as a sign of respect.[31]

> The use of one or more loaves of leavened bread for the Eucharist ceased, and small round wafers were substituted.

There was also a shift in terminology. Formerly the blessed bread had been referred to as offering, *oblatio*. But, in the west by the ninth century, it was referred to as victim, *hostia*. A shift also occurred in the east, and they referred to it as lamb, *amnos*.[32]

It was the end of the Middle Ages before these practices were adopted by most of the western church.

Two Restrictions. In the thirteenth century two more changes occurred which further hindered people from receiving holy communion. One was that a person was to go to confession prior to each reception of the Eucharist. The other was that married lay people were not to engage in sexual relations before receiving communion.[33]

East vs. West. The change to unleavened bread further accelerated the rift between the west and the east. Around the time of the Great Schism (1054), use of "unleavened hosts" was considered an offense against the faith. In the east, the leaven symbolized Christ's soul; to be without leaven would have meant to be without life. Later on, though, this criticism subsided.[34]

The various councils that attempted to heal the rift had to deal with the question of leavened-vs.-unleavened altar bread. For example, the Council of Florence in 1439 said, "The Body of Christ is truly consecrated with wheaten bread, whether leavened or unleavened; priests must consecrate the Lord's body in one or other of these ways, each following the practice of his own Church, whether Western or Eastern."[35]

V. *Contemporary Practices*

Wafers. Today, most Latin-rite Catholics and many other parishes and congregations in western Christendom use wafers for their altar bread. Baked from a batter containing only flour (sometimes white flour, sometimes wheat and white) and water, wafers tend to be small and thin and unfortunately, often have the consistency of styrofoam. In addition to the smaller wafers, many parishes use one large wafer so that the bread is more visible to the people. This large wafer is the one broken during the fraction rite.

In North America these wafers had formerly been baked in monasteries as a source of income. However, with the decline of the numbers of religious, more and more communion wafers are being baked by large, private firms called "altar bread agencies." They produce wafers under their own label or under the label of a formerly-baking monastery. Earlier in this century, according to Fr. Richard Reiser, some rural parishes actually had lay bakers prepare small numbers of wafers for their churches. Using "host presses," they baked the wafers four or five at a time on top of their cast iron stoves.[36] In Winnepeg, Manitoba there is an enterprising young woman who went into the wafer-baking business for herself after the religious sisters in that city ceased their baking. According to a July 4, 1988 televised news report, the woman mixes up the white-flour-and-water batter, scoops some of the batter onto a silvered grill, presses down with a silvered press, removes the large sheet from the griddle and rapidly punches out the wafers, one at a time, with a hand punch.

The fraction rite tends to be minimal in liturgies employing wafers as the communion bread. According to liturgist James Empereur, "As long as we do not use real bread, there is little hope for the restoration of [the fraction] rite. Once we use bread that is actually bread and not something that requires an act of faith that it is actually bread or something that can be distinguished from fish food, the fraction rite will return." [37]

Unleavened Bread. Flat, unleavened loaves (such as those recommended here) are used for holy communion in a small number of Latin-rite and Protestant parishes, although more often for holidays than regular Sundays. There are a number of Latin-rite Catholic parishes which tried using such bread in the past but have given up for various reasons: poor recipes, lack of quality control and ecclesial resistance among others.

Leavened Bread. Leavened bread is used exclusively for holy communion by most eastern Christians (such as the Orthodox churches and Ukrainian Byzantine rite), by some Protestant parishes, by African-American Catholic temples, and hardly at all by Latin-rite Catholic parishes. There are three main kinds of leavened altar bread: flat leavened loaves (sometimes used by Episcopalians), stylized bread (used to the exclusion of all others by eastern Christians) and ordinary loaves of bread used by everybody else.

Stylized leavened bread is a round loaf, about six inches wide and four-to-five inches high, with a special, elaborate scoring pattern on top (see Chapter 9). According to Father Theoharis Theoharis, they are sometimes baked by the clergy, and sometimes by lay people, although nominally these loaves are meant to be baked and offered by lay people exclusively.[38] If, as happens once in a long while, several families bring the bread, the presiding priest is required to consecrate at least part of each and every loaf brought. Also, some of the bread which is not consecrated, is simply blessed and then given out after the end of the liturgy proper to all who come up to receive it.

The fractioning of these elaborate loaves takes place during a ritual called the *proscomide*, in which the bread is cut up using a small knife, into at least three kinds of pieces: the "lamb" piece; pieces which commemorate the church triumphant, the church militant, Mary and other saints and angels; and the corner pieces which are not used (see diagram in recipe). The "lamb" piece is then cut up into smaller cubes, roughly one cubic inch to one cubic centimeter in size, and placed into the cup. Many eastern Christians practice intinction which is the receiving of the consecrated bread soaked in the consecrated wine.

Other Kinds of Bread. Some congregations, including at least one Lutheran parish near Washington, D.C., use store-bought whole-wheat pita bread. Many others, including many Baptist parishes, use store-bought crackers. John Wimber's Vineyard Christian Fellowship in Anaheim, California, uses Italian stick-breads. And, occasionally some budding liturgists (including my friends at Carleton College in the mid-1970s) have made well-intentioned attempts at baking whole-wheat-and-water "hosts." In the one instance I'm familiar with, the "hosts" — each the size of a small cookie — were as hard as rocks, and we crunched and giggled our way through holy communion.

[1] Joseph Stallings, *Rediscovering Passover: A Complete Guide for Christians* (San Jose, CA: Resource Publications, 1988), p. 138.

[2] Ibid., p. 304.

[3] Ibid., p. 233.

[4] Michael G. Lawler, *Symbol and Sacrament: A Contemporary Sacramental Theology* (Mahwah, NJ: Paulist Press, 1987), p. 129.

[5] Stallings, pp. 208-209.

[6] Ibid., pp. 279-280.

[7] Ibid., p. 282-283.

[8] Ibid.

[9] Ibid., p. 284.

[10] Ibid., pp. 288-289.

[11] Ibid., pp. 290-291.

[12] Ibid., pp. 304, 311.

[13] Ibid., p. 306.

[14] Josef A. Jungmann, S.J., *The Mass* (Collegeville, MN: The Liturgical Press, 1976), p. 131.

[15] Robert Cabie, *The Church at Prayer, Vol. II: The Eucharist* ed. A. G. Martimort (Collegeville, MN: The Liturgical Press, 1986), p. 79.

[16] Joseph Martos, *Doors to the Sacred* (New York: Doubleday & Co., 1981), p. 253.

[17] Stallings, p. 324.

[18] Cabie, p. 110, 84.

[19] Ibid., p. 77.

[20] Ibid., p. 82.

[21] Ibid., p. 80.

[22] Ibid.

[23] Phillippe Rouillard, "From Human Meal to Christian Eucharist" *Living Bread, Saving Cup,* ed., R. Kevin Seasoltz (Collegeville, MN: The Liturgical Press, 1987), p. 151.

[24] Cabie, pp. 77-78.

[25] Rouillard, p. 151.

[26] Cabie, pp. 143, 132.

[27] Rouillard, p. 153.

[28] Cabie, p. 143.

[29] Martos, p. 263.

[30] Cabie, pp. 135-136.

[31] Martos, p. 263.

[32] Jungmann, p. 50.

[33] Cabie, p. 138.

[34] Jungmann, p. 131.

[35] Cabie, p. 133.

[36] Telephone conversation with Father Richard Reiser, pastor of Saint John's Church of Clearwater, Nebraska, December 1990.

[37] James Empereur, S.J., *Exploring the Sacred* (Washington, DC: Pastoral Press, 1987), p. 139.

[38] Conversation with Father Theoharis Theoharis, pastor of St. Dionysius Greek Orthodox Church, Overland Park, Kansas, January 21, 1991.

Chapter 2

Qualities of Good Altar Bread

Here are some qualities that pertain to good altar bread:

>   - tastes good
>
>   - looks good, is big enough to be seen
>
>   - has few crumbs
>
>   - is fresh
>
>   - provides enough for everybody
>
>   - has no distracting ingredients

Tastes Good. When Jesus instituted and gave us the Eucharist, he knew we needed something tangible. That which can be tasted is tangible. The taste of food is important, even for spiritual food. Have you ever eaten a stale consecrated wafer during communion? Real presence, yes, but did it go down

easily? Probably not. It's important that the altar
bread blessed during Eucharist taste good.

Looks Good, Is Big Enough to be Seen.
Similarly, the visual appearance of altar bread is
important. Mass bread should look good and appear
fresh and tasty. The loaves should be round in shape
and thick enough to appear to be bread. The loaves
should be big enough to be seen by the those
assembled. Signs are meant to be seen. However, the
loaves shouldn't be so large that they're awkward to
handle. A four-and-a-half inch (11.5 centimeter)
diameter "round" works well.

Visibility. It is especially important to some
worshipers, particularly deaf worshipers[1] and
pre-literate children that the bread be large enough to
be seen and be readily identifiable as food. A real life
example of this: during the words of institution at a
Sunday liturgy, while the baked bread was being
elevated, a little girl blurted out, "Look Daddy, it's a
giant cookie!"

Has Few Crumbs. Many clergy, sacristans and
eucharistic ministers are seriously concerned about
the crumbiness of Eucharist Bread. This is
understandable. Many Christians, particularly
Catholic Christians, believe and trust in the real
presence of Jesus in the consecrated bread and wine.
Because of this, we show care in the way the
consecrated Eucharist bread and wine are handled.
That which was bread and wine is no longer just
bread and wine, but is now the Lord's own Body and
Blood — every last crumb and drop. Since the
handling and eating of sacred crumbs can be really

awkward, clergy and sacristans strongly prefer those altar breads which do not easily crumble.

Is Fresh. One way of assuring that the Eucharist bread tastes good is to make sure that it is fresh. And the best way to have fresh altar bread is to bake it right before the start of the service — "Just in Time Baking." Not only will the bread be fresh but it will also be warm. The aroma of the warm bread will waft around like incense and people will have one more reason to look forward to eating the blessed bread of the Eucharist. During the preparation time of a Mass in my former parish, the presider noticed that not only did the bowl of bread feel warm, but also that the inside of the bowl was steamy. It was then, he later confided, that he knew he was "in for a treat."

The next best thing after "Just in Time Baking," is to bake the bread ahead of time, wrap it thoroughly, refrigerate or freeze it. Right before the start of the service, heat it in a microwave oven until it's piping hot. In any case, it's best to not let altar bread sit exposed to air at room temperature for more than a couple of hours.

Provides Enough for Everybody. This can be accomplished with two considerations: have proper portion size and consecrate enough loaves. Each fragment has to be big enough to be chewed and savored. Scripture says, "Taste and see how good the Lord is." (Ps 34:9) and, "The one who feeds on my flesh and drinks my blood remains in me and I in him" (Jn 6:56).[2] The Lord's word in this matter is clear. After all, he didn't say, "Take and nibble...."

Likewise, there should be enough bread baked so that everyone can have a piece. The best way to ensure the quantity and size of the broken up pieces of Eucharist bread is to employ scoring.

Scoring

Scoring is carving indentations in the formed, but not yet baked, loaves (rounds) of altar bread. Scoring not only makes it easier to break the loaves during the fraction rite of the Eucharist, but it also helps to guarantee both a consistent size for each piece and a consistent number of pieces per loaf.

Some people say that scoring, while convenient, destroys the sign value. Others say that scoring actually enhances the appearance of each loaf — nicely-scored loaves often look like giant hosts (wafers). I score the bread.

In Chapter 4, directions are given for an 18-piece scoring pattern. Eighteen, in Hebrew, is a symbolic number meaning "fullness of life." I had been scoring this way for years — purely for practical and aesthetic reasons — when writer Joseph Stallings pointed out the symbolism involved.

Has No Distracting Ingredients. You may well have heard this apocryphal story about altar breads: One year an enthusiastic young religious educator led a group of confirmands, who were on retreat, in an exercise of baking bread for their retreat liturgy. During that liturgy, the presider, as was his practice, broke the loaves as he started to tell the institution story. While he was speaking, lo and behold, he spied a couple of raisins sticking out of the bread. He wound up saying, "This is my body...except for the raisins."

While many North American Christians love to eat a good nut, cinnamon or raisin bread, some of these folks have a serious problem with consecrating and eating that same bread during the Eucharist. Personally, I think that Jesus would love to bless such a bread himself. Even so, I shy away from ingredients which may make themselves unfavorably noticed: raisins, nuts, strong spices, and the like.

---

[1] According to M. Alverna Hollis, O.P., it is especially important to deaf worshipers that signs be large enough to be visible. See "What You Can Learn From Deaf Worshipers,"*Modern Liturgy* 15 (1988):8, p.18.

[2] According to the New American Bible, "the verb that John uses in this verse is not the regular verb 'to eat,' but a very realistic verb with a rather crude connotation of 'munch, gnaw.'"

Chapter 3

Baking Good Altar Bread

Here are six secrets for baking really good altar bread:

- pray

- avoid distractions

- use selective ingredients

- mix and sift thoroughly

- score with care

- avoid grit

Pray. In all seriousness, it's really important to be prayer-full when baking altar bread. There are three points to keep in mind.

First, try to avoid rushing. If you can't avoid rushing, at least try to feel calm as you bake quickly. Try to keep your thoughts focused on the Lord and how happy the people who are going to eat this bread will be.

Second, listen to recorded Christian music while you bake — it will set a prayerful mood and help you to stay calm. Note some suggestions included here.

My preferences include tapes of such mellow Catholic liturgical music as *In Your Presence* and *Salt of the Earth* by Ekklesia (Ekklesia Music Inc., Denver, Colorado), *Image of His Love* by Jackie Dicie (Resource Publications Inc., San Jose, California) and *No Greater Love* by Tom Kendzia (NALR, Phoenix, Arizona). During Advent and Christmas there's seasonal music such as *Gentle Night* by the Saint Louis Jesuits (NALR), and *Winter Grace* by David Haas and Jeanne Cotter (GIA, Chicago). Fran, my wife, on the other hand, prefers to listen to really upbeat music, e.g., *The Songs of the Vineyard* Sampler C.D. (John Wimber's Vineyard Christian Fellowship) and *Lord of Field and Vine* by Danny Consiglio (NALR).

Third, pray a short prayer over the ingredients while you mix and sift and over the oven while the loaves bake.

These three prayerful actions (avoiding rushing, listening to prayerful music and praying over the ingredients, dough and oven) help me to bake better bread more consistently (by calming me), make me more mindful of my fellow parishioners and enhance my prayer life.

Avoid Distractions. It's difficult for me to prepare altar bread at the same time as cooking supper or doing anything else. While the bread is in the oven, I usually stay in the kitchen and clean up the counter and wash the utensils (if not making more than one batch). By avoiding distractions, it's easier to not only remain prayerful, but also to avoid making mistakes.

Take heart though — some distractions can't be avoided. Once I even had to help someone check under the hood of their car while in the middle of baking altar bread for the Christmas Eve Masses. Because my hands became covered with motor oil, I had to scrub them carefully before resuming the baking.

Use Selective Ingredients. Wesson Sunlite Sunflower Oil works very well for me. When greasing the cookie sheet, I brush on enough oil to create a thick film to cover the entire sheet. When brushing flour off the loaves in the Wheat-and-Honey and Fran's-Wheat-and-Perrier recipes, I keep the brush oiled enough to thoroughly coat the loaves with oil as I go along.

I use Golden Blossom Honey which is a pure, low moisture, really good-tasting, mostly non-clover honey — it works well in the Wheat-and-Honey altar bread recipe. Pure clover honey not only imparts a somewhat harsh taste to the bread, the bread also tends to burn while baking. So I go out of my way to obtain Golden Blossom Honey.

Since Golden Blossom Honey is sold only in New Jersey and Pennsylvania, if you want to obtain it for baking altar breads there are three options: Write or call the maker — John Paton Inc., 73 East State Street, Doylestown, PA 18901, (215) 348-7050. (You can order a case of honey packaged in plastic squeeze bottles which ship well.) Beg your friendly grocer to

order it for you. Or, if you live close enough, drive to the nearest store that carries it. As an alternative, you can experiment with making a similar blend of honeys by mixing clover, sage, buckwheat and orange blossom honeys.

Mix and Sift Thoroughly. Thorough mixing and sifting of the bread mixture prior to baking helps ensure that each piece of each loaf will taste and look the same — good. You can even pray over the mixture while you're stirring and sifting it.

Score with Care. If you use the 18-piece scoring pattern suggested (see Chapter 4), be sure to center the inner circle and try to score the outer part into equal-size pieces. This way each loaf of bread will be consistently good-looking.

Avoid Grit. Try to avoid what I call grit: dried clumps of dough, extraneous loose flour, and crumbs. Grit clings to the top or bottom of the finished bread and causes it to be crumbly or it gets into the bread and causes that bread to be harder to swallow. You can avoid grit by taking these steps:

- Between loaves within a batch, rub, wipe or wash off excess flour and clumps of dough from your hands.

- Between batches clean the utensils used, and wipe the counter clean and recoat it with fresh flour.

- Also, fill a fresh glass with fresh oil, and wipe the cookie sheet clean of stale oil and crumbs (a paper towel works nicely).

Chapter 4

Wheat-and-Honey Bread

A half-batch makes four or five 18-piece loaves (72-90 pieces). A whole batch makes eight to ten 18-piece loaves (144-180 pieces).

Half-Batch	Whole Batch	
1 5/8 cups	3 1/4 cups	whole wheat flour
5/8 cup	1 1/4 cups	unbleached white flour
1 1/4 tsp.	2 1/2 tsp.	salt
1 1/4 tsp.	2 1/2 tsp.	baking powder
1 cup	2 cups	warm water
1 1/2 tbsp.	3 tbsp.	sunflower oil
1 1/2 tbsp.	3 tbsp.	Golden Blossom Honey

(Metric: 1 cup = 235 ml., 1 tbsp. = 15 ml., 1 tsp. = 5 ml.)

Note: You need about two additional cups wheat flour for rolling out the dough and about 3 more ounces sunflower oil for greasing the cookie sheets and brushing the loaves.

Estimated Total Preparation Time:

- 1 hour, 15 minutes for a half-batch (55 min. with practice)
- 1 hour, 30 minutes for a whole batch (1 hour with practice)
- 2 hours for two whole batches (if you overlap them)

Tools Needed:

- 2 medium-size (10 cup or 2.5L) mixing bowls
- small (4 cup or 1L) mixing bowl
- measuring spoons
- measuring cup set (and a separate 1-cup measure for the water)
- butter knife for scoring
- rolling pin
- 1-cup (250 ml) sifter
- basting brush or pastry brush (Brushes made with natural bristles more effectively brush off flour than those made with plastic, but an occasional bristle may come off onto the bread. It's good to set aside a brush just for bread-making.)
- small bowl or glass (4 oz.) to hold oil for brushing
- stirring ladle

- size 0, round, Rubbermaid Servin' Saver™ container (2 1/2 inch or 6.5 cm. diameter) — for scoring loaves

- size 1, round, Servin' Saver™ container (4 1/2 inch or 11.5 cm. diameter) — for stamping loaves

- cookie sheet: 14x16 inch (36x41 cm.) for a whole batch, 14x10 inch (25x36 cm.) for a half-batch. (Use of an insulated cookie sheet helps the bread bake more evenly and prevents burns.)

- metal spatula

- 2-4 paper-towel-covered dinner plates

- cassette tapes of Christian music and a player

Hints:

The lip of the Servin' Saver™ container shows if you rolled the dough to the right (1/2 inch or 1.2 cm.) thickness.

If you get fewer than 8, 4 1/2 inch rounds, you're probably rolling them too thick. If you get more than 10, you're probably rolling them too thin.

If you need to make more than 10 loaves (rounds), you'll get better results baking two or more separate batches instead of doubling the recipe.

Directions:

Start playing some Christian music and keep playing music until done. This helps set a prayerful and peaceful mood. Preheat the oven to 350 degrees F (180 degrees C).

Clean off a counter for mixing, stamping and scoring. After cleaning the counter, wipe once more with plain hot water — you will be putting flour and raw dough right onto the counter. As Julia Child would say, make sure your hands are "impeccably clean." Assemble all the bowls, tools and ingredients needed.

Measure wheat flour, white flour, salt and baking powder into one of the medium-sized mixing bowls and stir thoroughly. Sift dry ingredients three times: from the first bowl to the second, from second back to the first and once more from the first bowl to the second.

Measure warm water (as hot as it will come out of the tap) into the small mixing bowl — try to be precise. Measure honey into water one tablespoon at a time. Stir until dissolved. Measure sunflower oil into water. Stir until dissolved.

Add liquid mixture to dry ingredients in the medium mixing bowl and mix with ladle until all the floury mixture is gathered in — the dough will be sticky. If you can't seem to gather in all the flour after about 30 seconds of mixing, rinse the small bowl with two tablespoons of warm water and add that to the ungathered flour and stir again.

Sprinkle the counter with wheat flour — mainly to keep the dough from sticking to the counter. Pour the 3 ounces of sunflower oil into a small bowl or glass. Brush enough oil on the cookie sheet to thoroughly coat it. When in doubt, use more oil than not enough.

For the first loaf (round) of bread, do the following:

- Brush a little oil onto your hands.

- Place a handful of raw dough (about the size of a baseball) on the floured counter and sprinkle the dough with flour.

- Roll out 1/2 inch (1.2 cm.) thick and at least 4 1/2 inches (11.5 cm.) across.

- Follow the directions in "Stamp Out and Score".

- Save the scraps for use in the second loaf. If the first loaf (round) looks a little ragged, don't worry — that's to be expected.

- Using the spatula, carefully place the loaf (round) onto the cookie sheet. Try not to move the dough once it's on the sheet.

For each succeeding loaf (round) of bread, do the following:

- Rub, wipe or wash off the excess dough and flour from your hands.

- Brush a little oil onto your hands.

Stamp Out and Score

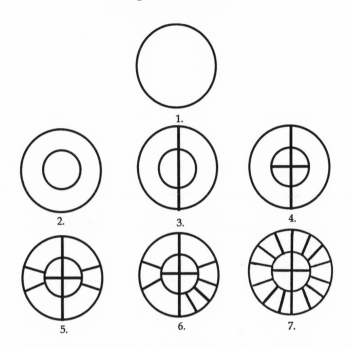

1. Stamp out a 4 1/2 inch (11.5 cm.) round using the size 1 Servin' Saver™ plastic container. Peel away the excess dough (scrap) and put it aside.

2. Deeply imprint with a 2 1/2 inch (6.5 cm.) circle using the size 0 plastic container — make sure it is centered.

3. With a butter knife or the dull side of a regular knife, score a vertical line through the center — deeply.

4. Score a horizontal line only across the inner circle — deeply.

5. Score the two side pieces — deeply.

6. Score deeply each remaining large corner section into three equal pieces.

7. Stamping and scoring completed.

· Take the scraps from the previous loaf and add to it some fresh dough. Form into a ball (about the size of a baseball). Make sure the fresh dough is on top and relatively free of wrinkles. Place the ball of dough onto the floured counter.

· Sprinkle the dough with flour. Roll dough out 1/2 inch (1.2 cm.) thick and at least 4 1/2 inches (11.5 cm.) wide and long.

· Follow the directions to stamp out and score.

· Using the spatula, carefully place the loaf (round) onto the cookie sheet. It's O.K. if the rounds just about touch each other, but not O.K. if they are squashed together. Try not to move the dough once it's on the sheet.

At the end, if there isn't quite enough dough to make a loaf, you can make one or more 2 1/2 inch (6.5 cm.) mini-loaves. Simply stamp them out with the size-0 Servin' Saver™ container and imprint the cross on them (imprint deeply).

Bake on a lightly oiled cookie sheet at 350 degrees F (180 degrees C) for 18 to 20 minutes (18 for half-batch). My ovens are electric and 18 minutes works well.

If you're baking more than one batch, start the next batch as soon as all of the first batch is in the oven. Make sure to clean the mixing bowl, rolling pin, and scoring knife and other bowls before reusing them. Also you may want to clean the old flour off the counter and sprinkle fresh flour on it.

Remove the cookie sheet from the oven. Lightly brush loaves with sunflower oil to remove the loose flour and add a nice color and texture. If in doubt, use more oil than not enough. Place the cookie sheet back into the oven. Bake 8 to 10 minutes more (8 for half-batch). In my oven, 8 minutes works best.

Remove the cookie sheet from the oven. Immediately transfer loaves to paper-towel-covered plates. This blots any excess oil and/or crumbs. Three rounds fit on one dinner plate — don't stack them. Blot for 3 to 5 minutes.

Sample a piece from one or two of the baked loaves to make sure it tastes good — this is important! If you're cooking a second batch, wipe the cookie sheet clean and re-coat it with fresh oil before placing any raw loaves on it.

If you're baking for a service (Mass) that starts in a little while, place the loaves, after they have been blotted, onto a platter or large plate using a clean spatula. If you're going to store these loaves for use at a later date, let the loaves cool somewhat and wrap and store according to the directions in Chapter 10. When done, turn off the Christian music and turn off the oven, too!

Chapter 5

Fran's Wheat-and-Perrier Bread

This recipe was devised by my wife, Fran, to satisfy a particular pastor. The trick is to use the fizz from Perrier, or some other non-flavored sparkling mineral water, in lieu of baking powder. Due to variances in the fizziness and apparent saltiness of mineral waters (even sodium-free waters), this recipe is not as foolproof as the preceding one. Note that by omitting the salt, oil, and honey from the dough mixture, this bread will meet the Latin-rite Catholic guidelines for Altar breads. A half-batch makes four 18-piece loaves (72 pieces). A whole batch makes eight 18-piece loaves (144 pieces).

Half-Batch	Whole Batch	
1 5/8 cups	3 1/4 cups	whole wheat flour
5/8 cup	1 1/4 cups	unbleached white flour
1 1/4 tsp.	2 1/2 tsp.	salt (see directions)
1 c. & 1 tbsp.	2 cps & 2 tbsp.	sparkling mineral water
1 1/2 tbsp.	3 tbsp.	sunflower oil
1 1/2 tbsp.	3 tbsp.	Golden Blossom Honey (optional)

(Metric: 1 cup = 235 ml., 1 tbsp. = 15 ml., 1 tsp. = 5 ml.,
1 cup & 1 tbsp. = 1 metric cup — 250 ml.)

Note: Allow for two additional cups wheat flour
for rolling out the dough and about 3 more ounces
sunflower oil for greasing the cookie sheets and
brushing the loaves.

Estimated Total Preparation Time:

- · 1 hour, 15 minutes for a half-batch (55 min.
  with practice)

- · 1 hour, 30 minutes for a whole batch (1 hour
  with practice)

- · 2 hours for two whole batches (if you
  overlap them)

Tools Needed:

- 2 medium-size (10 cup or 2.5L) mixing bowls

- small (4 cup or 1L) microwave-safe mixing bowl

- measuring spoons

- measuring cup set (and a separate 1-cup measure for the water)

- butter knife for scoring

- rolling pin

- 1 cup (250 ml) sifter

- basting brush or pastry brush. (Brushes made with natural bristles more effectively brush off flour than those made with plastic but an occasional bristle may come off onto the bread. It's good to set aside a brush just for bread-making.)

- small bowl or glass (4 oz.) to hold oil for brushing

- stirring ladle

- size 0, round, Rubbermaid Servin' Saver™ container (2 1/2 inch or 6.5 cm. diameter) for scoring loaves

- size 1, round, Servin' Saver™ container (4 1/2 inch or 11.5 cm. diameter) for stamping loaves

· cookie sheet: 14x16 inch (36x41 cm.) for a whole batch, 14x10 inch (25x36 cm.) for a half-batch. (Use of an insulated cookie sheet helps the bread to bake more evenly and prevents burning.)

· metal spatula

· 2-4 paper-towel-covered dinner plates

· cassette tapes of Christian music and a player

Hints:

The lip of the Servin' Saver™ container shows if the dough is rolled to the right (1/2 inch or 1.2 cm.) thickness.

If you get fewer than 8, 4 1/2 inch rounds, you're probably rolling them too thick. If you get more than 10, you're probably rolling them too thin.

If you need to make more than 10 loaves (rounds), you'll get better results baking two or more separate batches instead of doubling the recipe.

Directions:

Start playing some Christian music and keep playing it until done. This helps set a prayerful and peaceful mood.

Preheat the oven to 350 degrees F (180 degrees C). Clean off enough of a counter for mixing, stamping and scoring. After cleaning the counter, wipe once more with plain hot water. You will be putting flour and raw dough right onto the counter.

As Julia Child would say, make sure your hands are "impeccably clean." Assemble all the bowls, tools and ingredients needed.

Measure wheat flour, white flour, and salt into one of the medium-sized mixing bowls and stir thoroughly. Sift dry ingredients three times: from the first bowl to the second, from second back to the first and once more from the first bowl to the second.

Measure the Perrier, or some other non-flavored sparkling mineral water, into a microwave-safe cup or bowl, and immediately heat it on high for 45 seconds. If desired, measure honey into sparkling water one tablespoon at a time stirring until dissolved. Measure sunflower oil into sparkling water, and stir a few times — it emulsifies poorly in the sparkling water.

Add liquid mixture to dry ingredients in the medium mixing bowl and mix with ladle until all the floury mixture is gathered in — the dough will be sticky. If you can't seem to gather in all the flour after about 30 seconds of mixing, rinse the small bowl with two tablespoons of sparkling water and add that to the ungathered flour and stir again.

Taste some of the dough. If it tastes too salty, discard it and remake it with less salt or with no salt. Sprinkle the counter with wheat flour mainly to keep the dough from sticking to the counter. Pour the 3 ounces of sunflower oil into a small bowl or glass. Brush enough oil on the cookie sheet to thoroughly coat it. When in doubt, use more oil than not enough.

For the first loaf (round) of bread:

· Brush a little oil onto your hands.

· Place a handful of raw dough (about the size of a baseball) on the floured counter and sprinkle the dough with flour. Roll dough out 1/2 inch (1.2 cm.) thick and at least 4 1/2 inches (11.5 cm.) across.

· Follow the directions in "Stamp Out and Score," page 35.

· Save the scraps for use in the second loaf. If the first loaf (round) looks a little ragged, don't worry — that's to be expected.

· Using the spatula, carefully place the loaf (round) onto the cookie sheet. Try not to move the dough once it's on the sheet.

For each succeeding loaf (round) of bread:

· Rub, wipe or wash off the excess dough and flour from your hands.

· Brush a little oil onto your hands.

· Take the scraps from the previous loaf and add to it some fresh dough. Form into a ball (about the size of a baseball). Make sure the fresh dough is on top and relatively free of wrinkles.

· Place the ball of dough onto the floured counter.

- Sprinkle the dough with flour. Roll out 1/2 inch (1.2 cm.) thick and at least 4 1/2 inches (11.5 cm.) wide and long.

- Follow the directions in "Stamp Out and Score," page 35.

- Using the spatula, carefully place the loaf (round) onto the cookie sheet. It's O.K. if the rounds just about touch each other, but not O.K. if they are squashed together. Try not to move the dough once it's on the sheet.

- At the end, if there isn't quite enough dough to make a loaf, you can make one or more 2 1/2 inch (6.5 cm.) mini-loaves. Simply stamp them out with the size-0 Servin' Saver™ container and imprint the cross on them (imprint deeply).

Bake on a lightly oiled cookie sheet at 350 degrees F (180 degrees C) for 18 to 20 minutes (18 for half-batch). My ovens are electric and 18 minutes works well.

If baking more than one batch, start the next batch as soon as all of the first batch is in the oven. Make sure to clean the mixing bowl, rolling pin, and scoring knife and bowls before reusing them. Also, you may want to clean the old flour off the counter and sprinkle fresh flour on it.

Remove the cookie sheet from the oven. Lightly brush loaves with sunflower oil to remove the loose flour and add a nice color and texture. If in doubt, use more oil than not enough. Place the cookie sheet back into the oven. Bake bread 8 to 10 minutes more (8 for half-batch). In my oven 8 minutes works best.

Remove the cookie sheet from the oven. Immediately transfer loaves to paper-towel-covered plates. This blots any excess oil and/or crumbs. Three rounds fit on one dinner plate — don't stack them. Blot for 3 to 5 minutes.

Sample a piece from one or two of the loaves to make sure it tastes good — this is important! If it's too salty, and you used salt, start over and use less salt or no salt. Note that the bread produced from this recipe will not rise quite as much as that produced with the Wheat-and-Honey Bread recipe. If cooking a second batch, wipe the cookie sheet clean and re-coat it with oil before placing any raw loaves on it.

If you're baking for a service (Mass) that starts in a little while, place the now-blotted loaves onto a platter or large plate using a clean spatula. If you're going to store these loaves for use at a later date, let the loaves cool somewhat and wrap and store according to the directions in Chapter 10.

When done, turn off the Christian music and turn off the oven, too!

Chapter 6

Wheat-and-Water Only Bread

This bread is adapted from one created by
Deacon Bill Mallory of Hailey, Idaho. Bill is a
professional baker. Note that by omitting salt from
the dough mixture and by going easy on the oil when
brushing the loaves, this bread will meet the
Latin-rite Catholic guidelines for altar breads. Makes
five to six 18-piece loaves (90 to 108 pieces).

2 1/2 cups	whole wheat flour
1/2 cup	unbleached white flour
1 1/2 tsp.	salt (optional)
1 1/4 cups	warm water

(Metric equivalents: 1 cup = 235 ml., 1 tsp. = 5 ml.)

Note: Allow for one more cup wheat flour for
rolling out the dough and about 3 more ounces
sunflower oil for greasing the cookie sheets and
brushing the loaves.

Estimated Total Preparation Time:

- about an hour

Tools Needed:

- 2 medium-size (10 cup or 2.5L) mixing bowls

- measuring spoon (for salt)

- measuring cup set (and a separate 1-cup measure for the water)

- butter knife for scoring

- rolling pin

- 1-cup (250 ml) sifter

- basting brush or a pastry brush. (Brushes made with natural bristles more effectively brush off flour than those made with plastic but an occasional bristle may come off onto the bread. It's good to set aside a brush just for bread-making.)

- small bowl or glass (4 oz.) to hold oil for brushing

- stirring ladle

- size 0, round, Rubbermaid Servin' Saver™ container (2 1/2 inch or 6.5 cm. diameter) for scoring loaves

- size 1, round, Servin' Saver™ container (4 1/2 inch or 11.5 cm. diameter) for stamping loaves

· cookie sheet: 14x16 inch (36x41 cm.) for a whole batch, 14x10 inch (25x36 cm.) for a half-batch. Use of an insulated cookie sheet helps the bread to bake more evenly and prevents burns.

· metal spatula

· 2-4 paper-towel-covered dinner plates

· cassette tapes of Christian music and a player

Hints:

The lip of the Servin' Saver™ container shows if dough is rolled to the right thickness as it will allow up to 1/2 inch (1.2 cm.) of dough under it.

If you get fewer than 5 4 1/2-inch (11.5 cm.) rounds, you're probably rolling them too thick. If you get more than 6 1/2 rounds, you're probably rolling them too thin.

If you need to make more than 6 loaves (rounds), you can double the recipe, although you will have to increase the baking time to compensate. I don't recommend tripling the recipe.

Directions:

Start playing some Christian music and keep playing it until done. This helps set a prayerful and peaceful mood.

Preheat the oven to 350 degrees F (180 degrees C). Clean off enough of a counter for mixing, stamping and scoring. After cleaning the counter, wipe once more with plain hot water. You will be putting flour and raw dough right on the counter. As Julia Child would say, make sure your hands are "impeccably clean." Assemble all the bowls, tools and ingredients needed.

Measure wheat flour and white flour (and salt — optional) into one of the medium-size mixing bowls and stir thoroughly. Sift dry ingredients twice: from the first bowl to the second and from second back to the first. Measure warm water (as hot as it will come out of the tap) into the flour mixture — try to be precise.

Mix with ladle until all the floury mixture has been gathered in — the dough will be somewhat stiff. If you can't seem to gather in all the flour after about

30 seconds of mixing, measure 1/8 cup (60 ml) of warm water and add that to the ungathered flour and stir again. If that doesn't quite do it, add another 1/8 cup of warm water and stir again.

Sprinkle the counter with wheat flour mainly to keep the dough from sticking to the counter. Place dough on the counter or bread board and knead for about 5 to 6 minutes. If the dough is somewhat stiff, you probably won't need much extra wheat flour to facilitate the kneading. The kneading is important to prevent puffing or ballooning during baking.

When the dough is smooth and pliable, form the dough into a ball, cover it with a dampened clean cloth and let it rest for about 5 minutes. The cloth will prevent a crust from forming. Pour the 3 ounces of sunflower oil into a small bowl or glass. Brush enough oil on the cookie sheet to thoroughly coat it. When in doubt, use more oil than not enough.

At this point, choose "Tony's Variation" or "Bill's Original Recipe."

Tony's Variation

(small, scored rounds)

- Break the ball of dough into three baseball-size balls. For each loaf (round) of bread, do the following:

- Place a ball of raw dough on the floured counter, manipulate it until the top half of the ball is smooth and crevice-free, and sprinkle the dough lightly with flour.

· Roll out 3/8 inch to 1/2 inch (1.0 to 1.2 cm.) thick and at least 4 1/2 inches (11.5 cm.) across. This will be slightly thinner than the loaves in the preceding recipes.

· Follow the directions in "Stamp Out and Score," page 35.

· Using the spatula, carefully place the loaf (round) onto the cookie sheet. It's O.K. if the rounds just about touch each other, but not O.K. if they are squashed together. Try not to move the dough once it's on the sheet.

At the end, if there isn't quite enough scrap dough to make a whole loaf, you can make one or more 2 1/2-inch (6.5 cm.) mini-loaves. Simply stamp them out with the size-0 Servin' Saver™ container and imprint the cross on them (imprint deeply). Bake at 350 degrees F (180 degrees C) for 10 minutes.

If baking more than one batch, start the next batch now. Make sure to clean the mixing bowl, rolling pin, and scoring knife and bowls before reusing them. Also, you may want to clean the old flour off the counter and sprinkle fresh flour on it.

Remove cookie sheet from oven. Lightly brush loaves with sunflower oil to remove the loose flour. If in doubt, use more oil than not enough. Place cookie sheet back into oven. Bake bread 10 minutes more.

Remove cookie sheet from oven. Immediately break off a small piece from one or two of the two loaves and sample it. Is it acceptable? Some folks like it dry, almost like contemporary matzoh. And some like it somewhat chewy. If it's way too chewy, bake it for 3 to 5 more minutes.

Transfer loaves to paper-towel-covered plates. This will blot any excess oil and/or crumbs. Three rounds will fit on one dinner plate — don't stack them. Blot them for 3 to 5 minutes.

If cooking a second batch, wipe the cookie sheet clean and re-coat it with oil before placing any raw loaves on it.

If baking for a service (Mass) that starts soon, place the blotted loaves onto a platter or large plate using a clean spatula. If you're going to store these loaves for later use, let the loaves cool somewhat and wrap and store according to the directions in Chapter 10.

When done, turn off the Christian music — and turn off the oven, too!

Bill's Original Recipe

(large, unscored rounds)

· Break the large ball of dough into two smaller balls of equal size.

· Roll out each ball into an 8-inch (20 cm.) wide round about a 1/4 inch (0.6 cm.) thick. Neither the diameter nor the shape need be exact. If the rolled-out dough would fit nicely into the bottom of a pie plate, then the size is correct.

· Carefully transfer each round from the counter to the cookie sheet.

Bake at 350 degrees F (180 degrees C) for 16 to 17 minutes.

Immediately break off a small piece from one of the two loaves and sample it. Is it acceptable? Some folks like it dry, almost like contemporary matzoh. And some like it somewhat chewy. If it's way too chewy, you bake it for 3 to 5 more minutes.

Transfer the rounds to paper-towel-covered plates. This will blot any excess oil and/or crumbs — don't stack them. Blot for 3 to 5 minutes.

If you're cooking a second batch, wipe the cookie sheet clean and re-coat it with oil before placing any raw loaves on it.

If you're baking for a service (Mass) that starts in a little while, place the blotted loaves onto a platter or large plate using a clean spatula. If you're going to store these loaves for use at a later date, let the loaves cool somewhat. Then wrap and store according to the directions in Chapter 10.

When done, turn off the Christian music — and turn off the oven, too!

Chapter 7

St. Gregory's Abbey Altar Bread

This recipe, courtesy of Episcopal Father Robert Hutcherson of Raytown, Missouri, produces rounds of **leavened** bread which are tasty, chewy, slightly sweet and about an inch thick. Originally devised at the Episcopal Benedictine Abbey of Saint Gregory in Three Rivers, Michigan, this recipe has been slightly adapted here. As this recipe is truly leavened, it is unlikely any Latin-rite Catholic bishop would currently approve of its use. A batch makes about five 18-piece loaves (90 pieces).

at least 7/8 cup	warm water
3 tbsp	Golden Blossom Honey
1 1/2 tbsp	olive oil
at least 1/4 tsp.	salt
1 packet	dry yeast
2 2/3 cups	whole wheat flour

(Metric : 1 cup = 235 ml., 1 tbsp = 15 ml., 1 tsp. = 5 ml.)

Note: You'll also need one-half to 1 cup additional white flour for rolling out the dough and 2-4 more ounces of sunflower oil for oiling the baking sheet (and possibly for lightly brushing the loaves).

Estimated Total Preparation Time:

  · 2 to 2 1/2 hours

Tools Needed:

  · 1 small-size (6 cup or 1.5L) mixing bowl

  · measuring spoons

  · measuring cup set (and a separate measure for the water)

  · butter knife for scoring

  · rolling pin

  · clean cloth or towel

  · large spoon for stirring

  · size 0, round, Rubbermaid Servin' Saver™ container (2 1/2 inch or 6.5 cm. diameter) — for scoring loaves

  · size 1, round, Servin' Saver™ container (4 1/2 inch or 11.5 cm. diameter) — for stamping loaves

  · cookie sheet: 14x10 inch (25x36 cm.) or larger (a 14x10 sheet will hold up to 5 loaves, 14x16 up to 9). (Use of an insulated cookie sheet helps the bread bake more evenly and prevents burns.)

  · metal spatula

- pastry brush or a clean basting brush
- small bowl or 4 oz. glass for holding oil
- two paper-towel-covered dinner plates
- cassette tapes of Christian music and a player

Hints:

The lip of the Servin' Saver™ container (1/2 inch or 1.2 cm.) shows if you rolled the dough to the right thickness (1/4 inch or 0.6 cm. to 1/3 inch or 0.8 cm.).

If you get fewer than 4, 4 1/2 inch rounds, you're probably rolling them too thick. If you get more than 7, you're probably rolling them too thin.

When my wife, Fran, and I baked this bread, we found that although tasty, it could be improved with a little more salt and by lightly brushing loaves with oil 2/3 of the way through the baking process.

Directions:

Start playing some Christian music and keep playing music until done. This helps set a prayerful and peaceful mood.

Clean off a counter for mixing, stamping and scoring. After cleaning the counter, wipe once more with plain hot water — you will be putting flour and raw dough right onto the counter. As Julia Child would say, make sure your hands are "impeccably clean." Assemble all the bowls, tools and ingredients needed.

Measure warm water into the small mixing bowl and add yeast, stirring until yeast dissolves. Measure honey into water one tablespoon at a time. Stir until dissolved. Measure olive oil into water. Stir for a few seconds to break it up, but it won't emulsify much. Stir in the salt.

Add unsifted flour and mix with ladle until all the flour is gathered in — the dough will be somewhat stiff. If you can't seem to gather in all the flour after about a minute of mixing, add one tablespoon of warm water at a time until it does gather in. (When we tried this, it took 4 more tablespoons of water.)

Sprinkle the counter lightly with wheat flour — mainly to keep the dough from sticking to the counter. Turn the dough onto the counter and knead for 5 minutes. This kneading is important.

When the dough is nice and elastic, put into bowl, cover with a damp, clean towel, put in a warm place (e.g., on top of the 'refrigerator) and let rise for

60 to 90 minutes. The dough should double in bulk (from 3/4L to 1.5L). While the bread is rising, take a well-deserved break from all that kneading. But before you rest, clean off the counter.

Lightly sprinkle the counter with wheat flour — again, turn dough onto counter and knead for about a minute. Pour about an ounce of sunflower oil into a small bowl or glass. Brush enough oil on the cookie sheet to lightly coat it. (Since the dough is firmer than that produced by the Wheat-and-Honey recipe, you can go a little easier on the oil.)

Roll out the dough to between 1/4 (0.6 cm.) and 1/3 inch (0.8 cm.) thick and stamp out as many rounds as you can (follow the directions in "Stamp Out and Score" on page 35). Save the scraps for the next step. Note that the finished rounds will be about three times the thickness that you roll them out to.

Using the spatula, carefully place each loaf (round) onto the cookie sheet — they should be at least a half-inch apart. Try not to move the dough once it's on the sheet.

Form the scraps into a ball (try to make it relatively free of wrinkles) and reroll to the same 1/4 (0.6 cm.) to 1/3 inch (0.8 cm.) thickness. If you can stamp out a 4 1/2 inch loaf from the remaining dough, do that. Otherwise make one or more 2 1/2 inch (6.5 cm.) mini-loaves. Simply stamp them out with the size-0 Servin' Saver container and imprint the cross on them (imprint deeply) using the smaller of the two Servin' Saver containers.

Preheat the oven to 350 degrees F (180 degrees C).

Let the rounds rise for 10 to 15 minutes (on top of the oven, if possible, to make use of the warmth).

If you desire "unbrushed loaves," bake at 350 degrees F (180 degrees C) for 10 to 12 minutes. For "lightly brushed" loaves, bake for 7-8 minutes. Remove from oven, lightly brush the loaves with sunflower oil, place back in oven and bake for another 4-5 minutes.

If wish to experiment, try brushing two of the loaves so that you can compare the brushed loaves with the unbrushed ones. If baking more than one batch, start the next batch now. Make sure to clean the mixing bowl, rolling pin, and scoring knife and other bowls before reusing them. Also clean the old flour off the counter and sprinkle fresh flour on it.

Remove the cookie sheet from the oven and immediately transfer loaves to paper-towel-covered plates. This blots any excess oil and/or crumbs. Three rounds fit on one dinner plate — don't stack them. Blot for 3 to 5 minutes.

Sample a piece from one or two of the baked loaves to make sure it tastes good — this is important!

If you're baking for a service (Mass) that starts soon, place the "blotted" loaves onto a platter or large plate using a clean spatula. If you're going to store these loaves for use at a later date, let the loaves cool and store according to the directions in Chapter 10.

When done, turn off the Christian music and turn off the oven, too!

Chapter 8

Gaelen's Bread

This recipe, courtesy of Gaelen Evans of Mission Hills, Kansas, produces rounds of bread which are lighter in color, a little sweeter and a little thinner than the other recipes in this book. A batch makes about five 18-piece loaves (90 pieces).

One Batch	Double Batch	
1 1/2 cups	3 cups	white flour
1/2 cup	1 cup	whole wheat flour
1 tsp.	2 tsp.	sugar
1 tsp.	1 1/2 tsp.	salt
3/4 tsp.	1 1/2 tsp.	baking soda (not baking powder)
2 tbsp.	4 tbsp.	shortening
5 oz.	10 oz.	warm water

(Metric: 1 cup =235 ml., 1 tbsp =15 ml., 1 tsp. =5 ml., 10 oz. =300 ml., 5 oz. =150 ml.)

Note: Allow about a half to one cup more of white flour for rolling out the dough.

Estimated Preparation Time:
- 1 hour

Tools Needed:
- 1 medium-size (10 cup or 2.5L) mixing bowl
- measuring spoons
- measuring cup set (and a separate measure for the water)
- butter knife for scoring
- rolling pin
- whisk
- large spoon for stirring
- size 0, round, Rubbermaid Servin' Saver™ container (2 1/2 inch or 6.5 cm. diameter) for scoring loaves
- size 1, round, Servin' Saver™ container (4 1/2 inch or 11.5 cm. diameter) for stamping loaves
- cookie sheet: 14x10 inch (36x41 cm.) or larger (a 14x10 inch sheet will hold up to 5 loaves, 14x16 inch, up to 9). Use of an insulated cookie sheet helps the bread to bake more evenly and prevents burns.
- metal spatula

- mushroom brush, pastry brush, or a clean basting brush (It's good to set aside a brush just for bread-making.)

- sheet of baking parchment (obtainable at a gourmet cooking supplies store) or wax paper for lining the cookie sheet (Baking parchment will get a lot less scorched than wax paper at 425 degrees.)

- cassette tapes of Christian music and a player

Hints:

The lip of the Servin' Saver™ container (1/2 inch or 1.2 cm.) shows if dough is rolled to the right thickness (about 1/3 inch or 0.8 cm.). If you get fewer than 4, 4 1/2-inch rounds, you're probably rolling them too thick. If you get more than 6, you're probably rolling them too thin.

Although this recipe can be doubled (the two batch measurements), tripling is too hard to work with.

Directions:

Start playing Christian music and keep playing it until done. This helps set a prayerful and peaceful mood.

Preheat the oven to 425 degrees F (220 degrees C).

Clean off a counter for mixing, stamping and scoring. After cleaning the counter, wipe once more with plain hot water — you will be putting flour and raw dough right on the counter. Also, as Julia Child would say, make sure your hands are "impeccably clean." Assemble bowls, tools and ingredients needed.

Measure the flours, sugar, salt and baking soda into one of the medium-size mixing bowls and stir thoroughly, preferably with a whisk (although a mixer will work). Cut in the shortening.

Measure warm water (as hot as it will come out of the tap) — try to be precise. Stir in well (until all the flour has been gathered in). If you can't seem to gather in all the flour within about 30 seconds of mixing, add one or two tablespoons of warm water to the ungathered flour and stir again.

Sprinkle the counter with white flour mainly to keep the dough from sticking to the counter. Briefly knead the dough. Line the cookie sheet with baking parchment or wax paper.

Roll out the dough about 1/3 inch (0.8 cm.) thick and stamp out as many rounds as you can. See " Stamp Out and Score," on page 35. Save scraps for the next step.

Using the spatula, carefully place each loaf (round) onto the lined cookie sheet. It's O.K. if the rounds just about touch each other, but not O.K. if they are squashed together. Try not to move the dough once it's on the sheet.

Form the scraps into a ball (try to make it relatively free of wrinkles) and reroll to the same 1/3 inch (0.8 cm..) thickness. If you can stamp out a 4 1/2 inch loaf from the remaining dough, do that. Or make one or more 2 1/2 inch (6.5 cm..) mini-loaves. Simply stamp them out with the size-0 Servin' Saver™ container and imprint the cross on them (imprint deeply) using the smaller of the two Servin' Saver™ containers.

Bake at 425 degrees F (220 degrees C) for 10 minutes. Note that the parchment paper may scorch a little (wax paper may scorch a lot).

If baking more than one batch, start the next batch now. Make sure to clean the mixing bowl, rolling pin, and scoring knife and bowls before reusing them. Also you may want to clean the old flour off the counter and sprinkle fresh flour on it.

Remove cookie sheet from oven and cool the loaves, preferably on a wire rack. Sample a piece from one or two of the loaves to make sure it tastes good — this is important!

After the loaves have cooled a little bit, lightly brush off any excess flour with either a mushroom brush, pastry brush or a clean basting brush.

If cooking a second batch, line the cookie sheet with a fresh piece of baking parchment or wax paper before placing any raw loaves on it.

If you're baking for a service (Mass) that starts in a little while, place the loaves onto a platter or large plate using a clean spatula. If you're going to store these loaves for use at a later date, let the loaves cool completely and wrap and store according to the directions in Chapter 10.

When done, turn off the Christian music — and turn off the oven, too!

Chapter 9

Greek Orthodox / Eastern Rites Bread

This recipe, courtesy of Greek Orthodox Father Theoharis of Overland Park, Kansas, produces round loaves of **leavened** bread which conform to the ancient, steadfast practice of the churches in the East (such as the Greek Orthodox church and the Ukrainian-Byzantine Rite Catholic church). The loaves produced by this recipe (about 5-6 inches in diameter and 4-5 inches in height) are somewhat larger and thicker than those produced by the other recipes in this book. The scoring is different, too. The eastern churches usually cut up the bread right during their divine liturgies, with a small knife.

I have included this recipe here both as a kind of study text and as an experimental recipe for non-Latin-rite readers of this book. Since this recipe produces truly leavened bread, it is unlikely any Latin-rite Catholic bishop would approve of its use at this time.

This recipe makes two loaves. The number of pieces yielded depends on how each loaf is scored.

5 cups	white flour
1 tsp.	salt
1 cake/packet	yeast
2 cups	warm water

(Metric equivalents: 1 cup = 235 ml., 1 tsp. = 5 ml.)

Note: You could possible substitute partially or completely whole wheat flour. Allow about 1 1/2 cups more flour for working the dough.

Estimated Total Preparation Time:

· 2 to 3 hours

Tools Needed:

· 1 large mixing bowl

· measuring spoons

· measuring cup set (and a separate measure for the water)

· stirring ladle

· "seal" or a butter knife for scoring

· two small cake pans (at least 5 inches [cm.] wide)

· some quality paper towels

· cassette tapes of Christian music and a player

Hint:

This recipe doesn't work well doubled.

Directions:

Start playing some Christian music and keep playing it until done. This helps set a prayerful and peaceful mood.

Clean off enough counter space for mixing and kneading. After cleaning the counter, wipe once more with plain hot water — you will be putting flour and raw dough right on the counter. Also, as Julia Child would say, make sure your hands are "impeccably clean." Assemble all the bowls, tools and ingredients needed.

Measure the flour, salt, and yeast into a medium-size mixing bowl and mix thoroughly either with your hands or with a ladle or large spoon. Measure warm water (as hot as it will come out of the tap) — try to be precise. Stir in well (until all the flour has been gathered in). If you can't seem to gather in all the flour in about 30 seconds of mixing, measure one or two tablespoons of warm water and add that to the ungathered flour and stir again.

Sprinkle the counter with white flour mainly to keep the dough from sticking to the counter. Knead the dough for five to ten minutes. Work in more flour (add up to a cup more). Let the dough sit in a warm place, covered with a clean damp cloth, for about an hour. Lightly sprinkle the two cake pans with flour. Divide the dough into two round masses and place one in each cake pan.

Either impress each loaf with the seal or score the loaf with a seal-like pattern (see the sample following) using a butter knife or the dull side of a regular knife. If you are using a seal, dip it into flour before impressing each loaf.

Let rise for another hour or so. After about 50 minutes of rising, preheat the oven to 350 degrees F (180 degrees C).

Bake at 350 degrees F (180 degrees C) for about an hour. Remove the pans from the oven. Lightly wipe off any residual flour/crumbs with a moistened paper towel (this also helps keep the bread moist).

Sample a piece from one of the loaves to make sure it tastes good — this is important!

If you're cooking a second batch, wipe the cookie sheet clean and re-sprinkle with fresh flour.

If you're baking for a liturgy that starts soon, place the loaf onto a platter or large plate. If you're going to store these loaves for use at a later date, let the loaves cool completely and wrap and store according to the directions in Chapter 10.

When done, turn off the Christian music and turn off the oven, too!

The Seal

Notice the three occurrences of IC · X · N · K (this stands for "Jesus Christ, Victor"). The middle occurrence is the "host" or "lamb" and is further broken up for holy communion. The top one commemorates the church militant and the bottom one, the church triumphant.

The triangle in the middle left commemorates Mary. The nine arrow markings in the middle right commemorate all the saints. Each arrow stands for a

saintly category: angels, prophets, apostles, martyrs and so on.

The four corner pieces they are present only to complete the circle. In Eastern observances, only the "host" is used for holy communion; the remainder is reverently eaten by the priests after the liturgy.

Chapter 10

Wrapping and Storing Altar Bread

Maximum Storage Times

- up to 4 hours, unwrapped and unrefrigerated
- up to 24 hours, wrapped but unrefrigerated
- up to 6 days, thoroughly wrapped and refrigerated
- up to 40 days, thoroughly wrapped and frozen

Wrapping the Bread. I wrap each loaf, after it cools somewhat, in a separate piece of Glad™ Microwave Wrap (made of heavy gauge, microwave-proof plastic) — and place all the wrapped loaves in a large (size 6, round) Rubbermaid Servin' Saver™ plastic container. Seven or eight loaves usually fit in one such container. The whole point of the thorough wrapping is to make sure that the loaves don't dry out in the refrigerator or freezer.

Defrosting. Unwrap what you need and then heat not more than three loaves at a time on a microwave safe plate at **medium** or **defrost** for 1 to 2 minutes per loaf. When done, each loaf is piping hot, as if just baked. Air-thawing and oven-thawing don't seem to work nearly as well.

Transporting Warm Bread. I usually place the unwrapped loaves on a platter or large plate, stacked not more than six high, and wrap it all with two sheets of microwave/plastic wrap—loosely, so that it can breathe. Then I go directly to the church before it cools down.

Chapter 11

Vestry / Sacristy Particulars

Percentages of Wafers and Baked Bread. Some parishes try to use 90 percent baked bread and 10 percent wafers. The wafers are mainly for those people who prefer to receive the Eucharist bread on their tongues (rather than in their hands), for those times when they run out of baked bread, for the bread they reserve in the tabernacle and for nursing home liturgies.

Breaking the Bread. A decision you will need to make is whether or not to break up most of the loaves ahead of time. Some ministers prefer to break up all the bread (except for one loaf) ahead of time because it shortens the service by two or three minutes. I myself, for those liturgies when I'm in charge, prefer to have all the bread broken during the fraction rite of the liturgy because that makes for a better sign.

Sacred Dishes. Good liturgical sense says to try to keep all the bread on the altar table on one plate if possible (see rubric no. 293 in Appendix A and rubric no. 12 "of Vessels" in Appendix B). One parish uses a

large clear glass or crystal plate or bowl for the main
paten/ciborium and matching, smaller clear
glass/crystal bowls for the other ciboria — even for
the ciboria kept in the tabernacle (ciborium is Latin
for food dish). Likewise, they use matching crystal
stemware for the chalices.

Using a large bowl works well if you break up
most of the loaves ahead of time. If you decide to
break the bread during the fraction rite, you can do
what I do: use a plate (paten). Specifically, I use a
clear glass serving plate that matches the crystal
stemware. Whatever kind of sacred dishes you
decide to use, make sure they'll stand up to repeated
washing.

Eucharistic Adoration
(If applicable to your confession)

For the past several hundred years, monstrances
(a display holder for a blessed communion wafer)
have been employed to prominently display the
consecrated bread during benediction rituals and
eucharistic adoration.

When implementing the use of baked bread in a
parish, there are two monstrance-related issues to
consider:

1) will a piece of the bread fit into the
monstrance, and

2) even if the piece of bread fits, will it be visible?

The point of using a monstrance is for people to
see the blessed bread (and therefore prayerfully gaze
upon the Lord).

I'd like to suggest two alternatives to the use of a monstrance. One is to prominently display a napkin (purificator) covered crystal bowl of the consecrated bread — let the bread be somewhat visible through the side of the bowl (the only down side to this is that, if exposed for several hours, the bread could dry out). The other option is to display a pile of unbroken, but consecrated loaves in a nice, covered crystal or glass cake holder.

Quality Control. It's very important to control the quality of breads to be consecrated during Mass or services — particularly if you make use of the services of a large number of bakers or of persons who bake infrequently. The taste, appearance and portion size should be relatively consistent from loaf to loaf, batch to batch, and liturgy to liturgy.

Prior to each Mass or service, one person needs to be in charge of this quality control—particularly someone with good liturgical sense and who is not afraid to eliminate a batch of not-up-to-snuff bread. At one parish, this responsibility, along with that of putting out the correct amount of bread and wine, was given to the sacristan.

Before using a batch of altar bread, taste a piece or two of it.

- · Does the bread taste good?
- · Is it too dry?
- · Is it cooked enough?
- · Does it crumble too much?
- · Does each loaf look O.K.?

· Does each loaf that will go on the altar look like it will stay intact while the presider is elevating or handling it?

· Are the loaves scored into too-small pieces (too-large pieces can always be broken in half)?

Keeping a Ready Supply. Some sacristans and bakers try to keep a one-to-ten loaf supply of baked altar bread in their home freezers for unforeseen circumstances. When a need for the bread comes up, they heat in a microwave until hot the necessary loaves and then they take them to the church. A large congregation might even consider keeping a small freezer and microwave right in the sacristy or parish complex for this very purpose.

Careful Handling. The bread produced by some of the included recipes, even after consecration, may leave a slight slippery coating on the fingers. Use caution when trying to lift chalices (particularly metal ones) after handling the bread. Failure to be careful might cause the chalice, full of consecrated wine, to slip out of your hands and spill on the altar table. (unfortunately, this has happened). And make sure any hands any hands which handle or fraction this bread are, as Julia Child would say, "impeccably clean."

Storing Consecrated Bread. In reserving (storing) the consecrated Eucharist bread for the sick and for adoration, there are three concerns: respecting the dignity of the Lord's real presence in the blessed bread, keeping the blessed bread from drying out and keeping the blessed bread from growing moldy.

At room temperature (70 degrees F or 22 degrees C) this bread, when not wrapped or reserved in an air-tight and close-fitting container, can partially dry out within several hours even if covered with a sacred napkin (purificator). If reserved in an air-tight and close-fitting container, this bread will stay tolerably moist even at room temperature (70 degrees) for about three days; at that time it may start to grow moldy. If this bread is reserved in an air-tight and close-fitting container at a lower temperature, 35 degrees F to 50 degrees F (2 degrees C to 10 degrees C), it will probably keep a week.

Bear in mind that the main purpose of reserving the Eucharist is to have it available to be eaten by the sick and dying. The second purpose is to have it available for public and private adoration. If your congregation celebrates the Lord's Supper every day, there is no reason why the consecrated bread should have to be kept longer than one day — you could renew the supply in the tabernacle every day. If your congregation celebrates the Lord's Supper only on weekends, then the bread will have to be preserved for up to a week.

Some parishes shy away from reserving consecrated baked bread for more than an hour or two; they pretty much reserve only consecrated wafers. A less demanding approach would involve replenishing the supply of reserved blessed bread every day or using a passively cooled (down to 50 degrees F or 10 degree C) tabernacle. It's ideal for the

sick (and daily Mass-goers) to be given the same consecrated baked bread shared with parishioners at the Sunday services.

Consecrated Crumbs. Any leftover crumbs of the blessed bread should be eaten *reverently*. This is better done **after** the liturgy rather than during it. This can be done by either picking them off the plate/bowl with the fingers or by wiping/rinsing them into a chalice partly filled with water (the water is then drunk). Take reasonable care not to wipe crumbs off your hands onto the floor.

Sanitation. In addition to having clean hands when handling or fractioning the bread, it is important to actually wash, with dish detergent and hot water, the sacred dishes after each use (remembering to carefully consume the crumbs first).

Disposing of Excess Bread. Ordinarily, if too much bread is consecrated, the excess should be eaten or reserved. When there is too much left, even after some of the excess is eaten or reserved, that excess bread should be disposed of reverently. In addition, if the reserved blessed bread dries out or otherwise spoils it, too, will need to be disposed of reverently.

A proper, traditional and scriptural way to do this is to bury it. The pastor, deacon, sacristan or eucharistic minister could bury it in the earth in a quiet part of the church grounds, or if necessary, in the back yard of his/her own home. (If the ground is frozen, consider burying the bread in a large indoor planter.) To avoid unintentionally scandalizing the faithful, this burial should be done discretely, privately and reverently.

Setting Up a Bread-Baking Ministry. Decide first if the bread is to be baked in advance or just before the liturgy. This affects the number of bakers needed. For Just-in-Time baking, it is unreasonable to expect one baker to make more than one batch for a Sunday morning service—but maybe not for an evening or afternoon service.

For each service:

1. Take the number of people expected to attend the service (Mass) and divide by the number of pieces produced per batch for the recipe selected (e.g., 162 for the Wheat-and-Honey recipe). The result is the total number of batches that need to be baked.

2. Work down the list of bakers and the number of batches they have agreed to bake until you reach the number of batches needed. (The next time bread is needed, start with the next name on the list.)

3. Contact these bakers and notify them of the service for which their bread is needed.

Upon recruiting people to fill each of the scheduling slots, you can give each one a kit of sorts:

- · a copy of this book

- · a size-1, round Servin' Saver™ container (about $1.00 U.S.)

- · a size-0, round Servin' Saver™ container (less than $1.00 U.S.)

- · if the recipe calls for honey, a small (12-oz.) jar of Golden Blossom Honey (about $1.50 U.S.) or some other suitable honey.

And, if you have both the ambition and the time, invite each new baker into your kitchen and demonstrate how to bake a batch of altar bread.

Chapter 12

Introducing Parishioners to Baked Bread

Although I myself have never actually stood in front of an assembly to herald the use of baked bread for holy communion, I've helped plan for it in several different places. Introducing the use of this bread works best when you brief the sacristans and eucharistic ministers **ahead of time** and when you **briefly** tell those assembled at the start of the service.

What to Say

This is a revival of an ancient, scriptural, long-standing tradition.

This will help people to experience Jesus' real presence in the Eucharist even more richly.

The pieces of bread are a little bigger than wafers; so it is necessary to chew before swallowing.

Although the bread used is relatively crumb-free, there may still be some crumbs. In deference to the Lord's presence, it would be better to discretely consume the crumbs rather than shake them onto the floor. For those Catholics who are reluctant to deal with crumbs, receiving on the tongue remains an option.

You can even mention that bread-baking provides yet another way for people to get involved in the liturgy. Tell your parishioners that Saint Augustine's mother would never have thought to go to Mass without bringing the bread.[1]

If the congregation has decided to use a mixture of wafers and baked bread, **briefly** mention how that will work.

What Not to Say

Don't go on and on about the crumbs. At a recent special liturgy, the priest "explained" about the crumbs for close to five minutes — right at the beginning of the communion rite. This takes away from the reverence.

Don't explain that this is an innovation, because it's not: The use of baked bread for holy communion is the restoration of an ancient practice.

---

[1] Cabie, *The Church at Prayer, Vol. II: The Eucharist,* ed. A.G. Martimort (Collegeville, MN: The Liturgical Press, 1986), p. 77.

Chapter 13

Large-Scale Baking

For the Eucharist of a church conference, my
wife, Fran, and I were hired to bake the altar bread.
Since the planners expected about 2,000 people to
attend this conference, Fran and I were asked to bake
enough bread for all of them — all 2,000. Talk about a
massive undertaking!

Using the Wheat-and-Honey recipe, we baked 12
batches which contained 107 18-piece loaves and 17
4-piece mini-loaves. Including shopping, kitchen set
up, clean up and wrapping, this project consumed
about 16 dedicated person-hours over four calendar
days.

I shopped on Sunday and we baked on Monday,
Tuesday and Wednesday. On Thursday we turned
the refrigerated bread over to the conference staffers
and the Eucharist was celebrated on Saturday.

The ingredients alone for this undertaking cost
about $28.00 US (in 1987):

- Four 5-lb. sacks wheat flour
- One 5-lb. sack unbleached white flour
- One 12-oz. tin baking powder
- One 26-oz. box salt
- Two 32-oz. bottles of sunflower oil
- Three12-oz. jars of Golden Blossom Honey
- One small bottle of dish detergent (for clean up)
- Three 100-sq. ft. rolls of microwave wrap
- Two rolls paper towel (for clean up)

We found that three consecutive batches were all we could do before tiring out. Each batch took about an hour — so long as we started a new batch while the prior batch was still baking. In other words, we overlapped them. And all the while we listened to Christian music (about 20 or 25 cassettes worth) and tried to be prayerful. It was hard to stay prayerful all the time, but we did try.

Hopefully, this tale of ours has given you some idea of what it is like to bake altar bread for 2,000 in case you need to do it.

Chapter 14

Altar Breads in the Future

Substantial Bread. I advocate a return to the use of "substantial bread" — baked by parishioners — for Holy Communion. This was the norm in the western churches for over 800 years, and is still the norm in the eastern churches. I think the use of substantial altar bread helps many to experience Jesus more fully in the Eucharist, more fully meets the requirements in the rubrics,[1] and makes for a much better sign.

The use of edible bread baked by **parishioners** involves more people in the week-to-week celebration of liturgy and is itself a powerful sign. According to liturgist Eugene Walsh, when people bake altar breads at home they need not bake using some "elaborate ritual like some Greek monks might use" but should bake the bread simply, well and honestly.[2]

Recipes. I recommend the use of flat, scored, quick-breads, because:

- They work well for those accustomed to wafers.

- They are not just edible, but tasty, without having to use yeast.

- They are almost as convenient as wafers as far as counting out pieces is concerned (not that convenience should be an overriding factor).

- The use of such bread could serve as a bridge, in the future, to the use of regular, leavened bread.

- Such bread is relatively faithful to what Jesus used, what the early Jewish church used, yet still looks and tastes like bread.

Leavened vs. Unleavened. This whole concern over leavened vs. unleavened bread appears to be a clash between notions of using bread which is the same as that Jesus used (or what people *think* Jesus used) and using bread which looks and tastes like bread to today's cultures. As we have seen, for the most part, there was no distinction in the West until the ninth century: the adoption of the use of unleavened bread was "associated with developments in eucharistic theology, eucharistic liturgy and eucharistic piety now seen to be incomplete or unbalanced."[3]

Baking by Sacrament Recipients. Another thought is that first communicants (with help from their parents and/or teachers) can bake the bread for their special day. This would restore a practice that Hippolytus encouraged. The same can be said for confirmands for their confirmation, ordinands for their ordination and couples for their wedding day. The practice is rich in symbolism (e.g., the joining together of grain to grain) and something that will be remembered for years afterward. And yes, Fran and I baked the bread—together—for our wedding liturgy!

Blessed are the Bread Bakers. Finally, I think we can carefully restore the old practice of naming, thanking and/or praying for the bread bakers. Here's a quote from a model "Prayers of the Prone" (Prayers of the Faithful) written by a medieval bishop in southern France: "We will pray today for the benefactors of this church, especially those who provide the blessed bread today...."[4] Even though St. Jerome didn't think much of this practice, I think it emphasizes the "priesthood of the faithful" and encourages more parishioners to get involved.

---

[1] More fully than wafers — which according to Canadian liturgist J. Frank Henderson "do not meet the criteria for altar breads that are set out in the rubrics of the renewed liturgy." J. Frank Henderson. "Eucharist Bread: Actual Food" *National Bulletin on Liturgy* 12 (1979):129.

[2] Conversation with Father Eugene Walsh, S.S., in Long Beach, California, June 1988. I don't think Fr. Walsh meant to criticize eastern practices at all, but that he didn't think folks (including me) should be "over-pious" when baking altar breads.

[3] Henderson, p. 131.

[4] Robert Cabie, *The Church at Prayer, Vol. II: The Eucharist* ed. A. G. Martimort (Collegeville, MN: The Liturgical Press, 1986), pp. 156, 82.

Appendix A

Latin-rite Catholic Rubrics

Included here are citations of portions of recent Catholic Church (Roman Rite) documents — the rules and guidelines which pertain to altar breads, reservation of the Eucharist and eucharistic dishes. The sections in bold were highlighted by the author as being especially important. Note the advice of Canadian liturgist J. Frank Henderson, "All the criteria set out for making Altar bread for the renewed eucharistic liturgy should be taken seriously and considered together."[1]

General Instruction of the Roman Missal (1970)[2]

Bread and Wine

281. Following the example of Christ, the Church has always used bread and wine with water to celebrate the Lord's Supper.

282. **The bread** must be made only from wheat and **must have been baked recently;** according to long-standing tradition of the Latin Church, it must be unleavened.

283. The nature of **the sign demands that the material for the eucharistic celebration truly have the appearance of food.** Accordingly, even though unleavened and baked in the traditional shape, the eucharistic bread should be made in such a way that in a Mass with a congregation the priest is able actually to break the host into parts and distribute them to at least some of the faithful. (When, however, the number of communicants is large or other pastoral needs require it, small hosts are in no way ruled out.) The action of the breaking of the bread, the simple term for the Eucharist in apostolic times, will more clearly bring out the force and meaning of the sign of the unity of all in the one bread and of their charity, since the one bread is being distributed among the members of one family.

284. The wine for the Eucharist must be from the fruit of the vine (see Lk 22:18), natural, and pure, that is not mixed with any foreign substance.

285. Care must be taken to ensure that the elements are kept in good condition: that the wine does not turn to vinegar or the bread spoil or become too hard to be broken easily.

Sacred Vessels

289. Among the requisites for the celebration of Mass, the sacred vessels hold a place of honor, especially the chalice and paten, which are used in presenting, consecrating and receiving the bread and wine.

290. Vessels should be made from materials that are solid and that in the particular region are regarded as noble. The conference of bishops will be the judge in this matter. But preference is to be given to materials that do not break easily or become unusable.

291. Chalices and other vessels that serve as receptacles for the blood of the Lord are to have a cup of non-absorbent material. The base may be of any other solid and worthy material.

292. Vessels that serve as receptacles for the eucharistic bread, such as a paten, ciborium, pyx, monstrance, etc., may be made of other materials that are prized in the region, for example, ebony or other hard woods, as long as they are suited to sacred use.

293. For the consecration of hosts **one rather large paten may properly be used;** on it is placed the bread for the priest as well as for the ministers and the faithful.

295. The artist may fashion the sacred vessels in a shape that is in keeping with the culture of each region, provided each type of vessel is suited to the intended liturgical use.

Third Instruction on the Correct Implementation of the Constitution on the Sacred Liturgy[3]

(Liturgiae Instaurationes, Sacred Congregation for Divine Worship, 5 Sept. 1970)

Bread and Wine

5. The bread used for the celebration of the Eucharist is wheat bread, and, according to the ancient custom of the Latin Church, is unleavened.

...Though the nature of the sign demands that **this bread appear as actual food which can be broken and shared** among brothers....

The necessity for the sign to be genuine applies more to the color, taste and texture of the bread than to its shape. **Out of reverence for the sacrament, every care and attention should be used in preparing the altar bread. It should be easy to break and should not be unpleasant for the faithful to eat.** Bread which tastes of uncooked flour, or which becomes dry and inedible too quickly, must never be used.

The breaking of the consecrated bread and the receiving of the bread and wine, both at communion and in consuming what remains after communion, should be conducted with the greatest reverence.

Environment and Art in Catholic Worship

(National Conference of Catholic Bishops (U.S.), 1978)

Environment and Art in Catholic Worship is written in clear, understandable English. Another reason is that it gives a vision of how powerful and beautiful liturgy should be. If you can obtain a copy of it, examine closely paragraphs 14, 15, 8-87.

These rubrics point out that liturgical signs (words, gestures, movements, objects, furnishings, art, etc.) need to be real, personal, and genuine (not phony) and certainly not minimalized. All signs need to be "opened up." it says, and five signs in particular: bread, wine, water, oil and the laying on of hands.

Liturgical objects, it goes on, should not be only rubrically "suitable" but should also make sensory contributions to the beauty of the worship, visually and otherwise (they don't give an example for "otherwise" but two that come to mind are the smells of fresh-baked bread and burning incense).

Finally, the rubrics stress that when going all out to renew and enrich the liturgy, the bread and wine cannot be ignored. These central symbols must be fully expressed even if that is "less efficient."

Instruction on Eucharistic Worship[4]
(Eucharisticum Mysterium, The Sacred Congregation
of Rites,1967)

3e. The celebration of the Eucharist in the sacrifice of the Mass is the origin and consummation of the worship shown to the Eucharist outside Mass. Not only are the sacred species which remain after Mass derived from the Mass, but they are preserved so that those of the faithful who cannot come to Mass may be united to Christ and His Sacrifice celebrated in the Mass, through sacramental Communion received with the right dispositions.

Consequently the Eucharistic sacrifice is the source and the summit of the whole of the Church's worship and of the Christian life. The faithful participate more fully in this sacrament of thanksgiving, propitiation, petition and praise, not only when they wholeheartedly offer the Sacred Victim, and in it themselves, to the Father with the priest, but also when they receive this same Victim sacramentally.

3f. There should be no doubt in anyone's mind "that all the faithful ought to show to this most holy sacrament the worship which is due to the true God, as has always been the custom of the Catholic Church. Nor is it to be adored any the less because it was instituted by Christ to be eaten. " For even in the reserved sacrament He is to be adored because He is substantially present there....

4. ...The particular purpose of these rules is not only to emphasize the general principles of how to instruct the people in the Eucharist, but also to make more readily intelligible the signs by which the Eucharist is celebrated as the memorial of the Lord and worshiped as a permanent sacrament in the Church.

For although this sacrament has this supreme and unique feature, that the author of holiness is Himself present in it, nevertheless, in common with the other sacraments, it is the symbol of a sacred reality and the visible form of an invisible grace. **Consequently the more intelligible the signs by which it is celebrated and worshiped, the more firmly and effectively it will enter into the minds and lives of the faithful.**

[1] J. Frank Henderson. "Eucharist Bread: Actual Food" *National Bulletin on Liturgy* 12 (1979):143.

[2] Selections from *The Roman Missal* (INternational Commission on English in the Liturgy, Inc., 1973).

[3] Selections from "Third Instruction on the Correct Implementation of the Constitution on the Sacred Liturgy," *Vatican II: The Conciliar and Post Conciliar Documents,* (Northport, NY: Costello Publishing Co., 1975).

[4] Selections from "Instruction on Eucharistic Worship," *Vatican II: The Conciliar and Post Conciliar Documents,* (Northport, NY: Costello Publishing Co., 1975).

Appendix B

Episcopal "Rubrics"

According to liturgist Robert Hutcherson, there are no Episcopal canonical rubrics, per se, concerning ingredients for altar breads and only a few concerning the handling of altar breads. Episcopalians, according to Fr. Hutcherson, obtain guidance concerning these matters

· by examining the living tradition of the church as revealed in the *Book of Common Prayer* and in current practice,

· by examining the writings of prominent liturgists, and

· by examining the canons and current practices of the Latin Rite Church.

Although both leavened and unleavened breads are widely used, Hutcherson notes the practical considerations associated with eucharistic reservation seem to favor breads which keep well at room temperature for several days. Another consideration is the widespread practice of intinction: the dipping of pieces of substantial consecrated bread into the wine is awkward at best.

For these reasons, most Episcopal parishes use either wafers or a mixture of wafers and substantial breads. Where mixtures are used, the wafers are mainly used for intinction and reservation. Hutcherson says his parish uses a mixture of substantial bread and wafers. He points out that the Anglican tradition does not prohibit the use of either yeast or of sweeteners, such as honey, in altar breads.[1] (The recipe his parishioners use, the "St. Gregory's Abbey Altar Bread" recipe, can be found in Chapter 7.)

Some passages from *The Ceremonies of the Eucharist,* by Howard Galley, a book recommended by Hutcherson, follow:

Of the Preparation of the Table

"...The recommendation of the Prayer Book (*Book of Common Prayer*) is that only one chalice be placed on the altar at the offertory (p. 407). Additional wine, if needed, is to be consecrated in a flagon or cruet. It is also desirable that there be only one paten, and that it be large enough to hold all the bread to be consecrated."

3. Of the Bread and Wine

"Anglicanism has faithfully adhered to the tradition of the undivided church that the bread to be used at communion be made from wheat flour and

that the wine be made from grapes. The bread may
be leavened or unleavened.[2]

"Since the use of a single loaf of bread is
obviously a more powerful symbol of the "one
bread" spoken of in the New Testament (1 Cor 10:17),
it is the practice recommended here. When wafer
bread is used, it is recommended that large
whole-wheat ones be used exclusively, each being
broken (at the proper time) into several pieces. If, at
very large services, individual wafers are preferred, it
is suggested that three or four large ones be
consecrated as well, so that all may see a significant
amount of bread being broken."

4. Of the Presentation of the Offerings

"...As a careful look at the rubrics will show, it is
not the intention of the Prayer Book to introduce a
'transfer of the gifts' of the eastern kind (p. 361). The
intention, rather is to underscore the fact that the
bread and wine are offerings of the people, products
both of nature (of which we are God's appointed
stewards) and of human labor.

"The ceremonial suggested in this book is
therefore wholly practical and functional:
representative lay members of the congregation bring
forward the bread and wine at the same time as
others bring forward the money and other gifts.[3]

"...If, as recommended, the bread presented is a
loaf, it may be brought forward on the paten on
which it will be consecrated, or in a convenient
basket."[4]

18. Of the Anthem at the Breaking of the Bread

"...It should be noted that the Prayer Book, following what was once the universal tradition of the church, expects that all who communicate at the eucharist will receive bread and wine consecrated at that celebration. **It does not anticipate that any will be communicated from the reserved sacrament, or that what remains of the reserved species when a fresh supply is reserved will be used to communicate persons at a subsequent eucharist.**"

23. Of the Reverent Consumption of What Remains

"Anglican Prayer Books since 1662 have specifically required that any consecrated bread and wine not needed for communion be reverently consumed by the priest and other communicants.[5]

"...The present Prayer Book specifies that the reverent consuming of what remains of the sacramental species take place "either after the Communion of the people or after the Dismissal" (pp. 408-409). It also...provides for the reservation of any needed portion of it.

"The Prayer Book also provides that deacons may 'remove the vessels from the Altar, consume the remaining Elements, and cleanse the vessels in some convenient place' (p. 555)."[6]

Of the Reservation of the Sacrament

169. The Prayer Book provides for the reservation of the consecrated elements for three purposes: 1. For the communion of individuals who cannot be present at a public celebration of the eucharist. 2. For the communion of a congregation in the absence of a priest. 3. For communion on Good Friday, from the sacrament consecrated at the Maundy Thursday liturgy."[7]

"...In some cases, the reservation is of bread only, and in others, of both kinds. Both practices can claim ancient precedent.

"It is strongly recommended that the bread to be reserved not be consecrated in a ciborium. The Prayer Book prefers that there be only one chalice on the altar during the eucharistic prayer, and ciboria look too much like chalices not to cause visual confusion...."[8]

"...The amount of bread and wine reserved should not exceed what may reasonably be expected to be needed, and this supply should be renewed on a periodic basis. This is especially true of the wine, which spoils easily.

"The most convenient way of doing this is to own two sets of vessels for reservation. The set containing the freshly consecrated species having been placed in the aumbry after communion, the other set can then be removed, the contents reverently consumed, and the vessels cleansed, either immediately, or after the service."[9]

12. Of Vessels

"Chalices are commonly made of precious metals, or at least plated with such metals. Other materials, such as glass or ceramic, are also suitable, provided they are not porous. As the most

conspicuous of the sacred vessels, it is desirable that
chalices be well designed and finely crafted. It is also
important that they not be top-heavy."[10]

"Patens intended for wafer bread ('well' patens)
are usually designed to fit on top of the chalice,
which is a convenience when bringing the vessels to
the altar at the offertory. Patens intended for
leavened bread are, of necessity, considerably larger,
as well as being deeper. They also may be made of
any suitable material. It is desirable that the paten
used be large enough to hold all the bread to be
consecrated at the service. When necessary,
additional patens can be brought to the altar at the
time of the breaking of the bread and used in the
distribution of communion.

"Flagons are pitcher-like vessels, frequently with
hinged covers, used to hold additional wine to be
consecrated at the celebration. Like chalices, it is
important that they be made of a non-porous
material. In some places, the people's offering of wine
is brought to the altar in a flagon, which is then used
to fill the chalice. An attractive carafe or decanter
may be used instead."[11]

7. Of the Place of Reservation

"The Prayer Book (p. 408) provides for the
reservation of the consecrated sacrament...where the
consecrated species may be 'kept in safety.'

"...It is desirable that the tabernacle or aumbry
be large enough to accommodate two sets of vessels
containing the sacrament.

"It is important that the aumbry or tabernacle not dominate the place of worship. In the course of the liturgy, the presence of Christ is manifested in various ways: in the midst of the people gathered in Christ's name, in the reading and proclamation of the word, in the persons of those who minister in various ways, and finally, under the species of bread and wine. It is difficult for worshipers to experience and appreciate these various modes of presence if the place of reservation is so centrally located as to constantly call attention to itself, as inevitable when a tabernacle is located on or behind the altar.

"The following is therefore recommended: ...When possible, the place of reservation should be in a separate chapel or room...attractively decorated, and conducive to private prayer and meditation. If the chapel contains an altar where weekday or early services take place, it is recommended that the aumbry be located in a side wall of the chancel [of that chapel]...."[12]

[1] Conversation with Father Robert Hutcherson, rector of Saint Matthew's Episcopal Church in Rayton, Missouri, March 1, 1991.

[2] Howard E. Galley, *The Ceremonies of the Eucharist: A Guide for Celebration* (Cambridge, MA: Cowley Publications, 1989)., p. 101.

[3] Ibid., p. 102.

[4] Ibid., p. 103.

[5] Ibid., p. 125.

[6] Ibid., p. 126.

[7] Ibid., p. 192.

[8] Ibid., p. 193.

[9] Ibid., p. 194.

[10] Ibid., p. 15.
[11] Ibid., p. 16.
[12] Ibid., p. 7.

Quick Reference Pull-out Recipes

Wheat-and-Honey Bread

Half-Batch	Whole Batch	
(4-5 18 piece loaves)	(8-10 18 piece loaves)	
1 5/8 cups	3 1/4 cups	whole wheat flour
5/8 cup	1 1/4 cups	unbleached white flour
1 1/4 tsp.	2 1/2 tsp.	salt
1 1/4 tsp.	2 1/2 tsp.	baking powder
1 cup	2 cups	warm water
1 1/2 tbsp.	3 tbsp.	sunflower oil
1 1/2 tbsp.	3 tbsp.	Golden Blossom Honey

(Plus additional wheat flour and sunflower oil)

Mixing Ingredients

Preheat oven to 350 degrees F (180 degrees C). Measure and mix dry ingredients. Sift 3 times. Measure hot tap water into small mixing bowl. Add honey to water — 1 T. at a time. Stir until dissolved. Measure sunflower oil into water. Stir until dissolved. Add liquids. Mix —dough will be sticky. If dry, add 2 tblsp. warm water and stir. Roll out dough and stamp/score. Bake on a lightly oiled cookie sheet at 350 degrees F (180 degrees C) for 18-20 min. Remove from oven. Lightly brush loaves with oil. Return to oven. Bake 8-10 min more. Remove from oven. Transfer loaves to paper-towel-covered plates. Blot 3-5 min. Sample a piece to make sure it tastes good. If using immediately, place on a platter. Cover loosely for transport. If storing,Cool loaves. Wrap each loaf loosely in microwave wrap. Place in a plastic container. Refrigerate or freeze.

Fran's Wheat-and-Perrier Bread

Half-Batch (4 18 piece loaves)	Whole Batch (8 18 piece loaves)	
1 5/8 cups	3 1/4 cups	whole wheat flour
5/8 cup	1 1/4 cups	unbleached white flour
1 1/4 tsp	2 1/2 tsp	salt (see directions)
1 cup, 1 tbsp.	2 cups, 2 tbsp.	unflavored sparkling mineral water
1 1/2 tbsp.	3 tbsp.	sunflower oil
1 1/2 tbsp.	3 tbsp.	Golden Blossom Honey (optional)

Preheat oven to 350 degrees F (180 degrees C). Gather bowls, tools, and ingredients. Measure and mix dry ingredients. Sift three times. Measure Perrier or other unflavored sparkling mineral water into microwave-safe bowl. Heat on **high for 45 seconds**. (Optional: Measure honey into sparkling water 1 tablespoon at a time until dissolved.) Measure oil into water, stirring. Add liquids to dry ingredients. Mix—dough will be sticky. If dry, add 2 tblsps. warm water and stir again. Taste dough. If too salty, discard and remake with less or no added salt. Form loaves.

Bake on a lightly oiled cookie sheet at **350 degrees F** (180 degrees C) for 18-20 min. Remove from oven and brush with oil. Return to oven. Bake 8-10 min more. Remove from oven. Transfer loaves to paper-towel-covered plates. Blot 3-5 min. Sample a piece to check taste. If using immediately, place loaves on a platter. Cover loosely if needed for transport. If storing, cool loaves. Wrap each loaf loosely in microwave wrap. Store in a plastic container. Refrigerate or freeze.

(Metric equivalents: 1 cup = 235 ml, 1 tbsp. = 15 ml, 1 tsp = 5 ml, 1 cup, 1 tbsp. = 1 metric cup [250 ml])

Wheat-and-Water Only Bread

Makes five or six 18 piece loaves.

2 1/2 cups	whole wheat flour
1/2 cup	unbleached white flour
1 1/2 tsp.	salt (optional)
1 1/4 cups	warm water

Preheat oven to 350 degrees F (180 degrees C). Gather bowls, tools, and ingredients. Measure and mix dry ingredients. Sift twice. Measure hot tap water into small mixing bowl. Add liquids. Mix—dough will be sticky. If dry, add 1/8 cup (60 ml) warm water. Stir. If necessary, add 1/8 cup more water and stir.Dust counter with flour. Knead dough 5-6 minutes. When dough is smooth, form a ball, cover it with a dampened cloth, and let it rest 5 min. Coat cookie sheet with oil.

Tony's Variation *(small scored rounds)*

Separate dough into 3 baseball-size balls of dough.Take 1 ball, smooth it and sprinkle lightly with flour. Roll out 3/8 - 1/2 inch (1.0-1.2 cm) thick and 4 1/2 inches (11.5 cm) round. Stamp out a 4 1/2 inch (11.5 cm) circle. Save scraps. Deeply imprint a 2 1/2 inch (6.5 cm) circle in the center. Score vertically through center. Score inner circle horizontally. Score deeply 6 sections on each side of vertical score.Transfer loaf to cookie sheet with spatula. Use scraps to make some 2 1/2 inch (6.5 cm) loaves. Stamp with circle and imprint cross on each.Start preparing the next batch.

Bake at 350 degrees F (180 degrees C) for **10 min.**. Remove from oven. Lightly brush loaves with oil. Return to oven. Bake 10 min. more. Remove from oven. Sample for taste and chewiness. If too chewy, bake **3-5 min. more.** Transfer loaves to paper-towel-covered plates. Blot 3-5 min.

Bill's Original Recipe *(large, unscored rounds)*

eparate dough into 2 equal balls.Roll each ball out 1/4 in. (0.6 cm) thick and 8 in. (20 cm) across. Place each round onto cookie sheet. If baking more than 1 batch, start preparing the next batch as soon as first batch is in oven. Bake at **350 degrees F** (180 degrees C) for **16-17 min.**. Remove from oven. Sample taste and chewiness. If too chewy, bake 3-5 min. more. Transfer loaves to paper-towel-covered plates. Blot 3-5 min. If using immediately, place loaves on a platter. Cover loosely for transport. If storing, cool loaves. Wrap each loaf loosely in microwave wrap. Place in a plastic container. Refrigerate or freeze.

(Metric equivalents: 1 cup = 235 ml, 1 tsp = 5 ml)

Gaelen's Bread

One Batch (5 18 piece loaves)	Double Batch (10 18 piece loaves)	
1 1/2 cups	3 cups	white flour
1/2 cup	1 cup	whole wheat flour
1 tsp.	2 tsp.	sugar
1 tsp.	1 1/2 tsp	salt
3/4 tsp.	1 1/2 tsp.	baking soda
2 tbsp.	4 tbsp.	shortening
5 oz.	10 oz.	warm water

Preheat oven to **425 degrees** F (220 degrees C). Measure dry ingredients. Stir with whisk or mixer. Cut in shortening. Measure hot tap water and add to dry ingredients. Dust counter with flour. Briefly knead dough. Line cookie sheet with baking parchment or wax paper. Roll out dough 1/3 in. (0.8 cm) thick and stamp as many rounds as you can.

If baking more than one batch, start next batch as soon as first batch is in oven. Bake at **425 degrees** F (220 degrees C) for **10 minutes**. (Parchment may scorch some; wax paper may scorch a lot.) Remove from oven. Sample a piece to make sure it tastes OK. After cooling, brush off excess flour with mushroom brush or pastry brush. Place loaves on a platter. Cover loosely if needed for transport. If storing, cool loaves. Wrap each loaf loosely in microwave wrap. Place all loaves in a plastic container. Refrigerate or freeze.

(Metric equivalents: 1 cup = 235 ml, 1 tbsp. = 15 ml, 1 tsp = 5 ml, 5 oz., = 150 ml, 10 oz. = 300 ml)

Greek Orthodox/Eastern Rites Bread

This recipe makes two loaves. The number of pieces yielded depends on how each loaf is scored.

5 cups	white flour
1 tsp.	salt
1 cake/packet	yeast
2 cups	warm water

Measure dry ingredients and mix thoroughly. Measure hot tap water into small mixing bowl. Mix—dough will be sticky. If dry, add 2 tblsp warm water and stir again. Dust counter with flour. Knead dough 5-10 min. Work in more flour (up to 1 cup). Cover dough with damp cloth, let sit in warm place, about 1 hr. Sprinkle 2 cake pans with flour. Divide the dough between pans. Impress each loaf with a "seal" or score with seal-like pattern using a butter knife or dull side of a regular knife. (If using a "seal," dip it into flour before impressing each loaf.) Let dough rise another hour. Let rise.

Preheat oven to **350 degrees F** (180 degrees C). Bake loaves for **1 hour**. Remove from oven. Lightly wipe off excess flour/crumbs with moistened paper towel. Place loaves on a platter. Cover loosely for transport. If storing, cool loaves. Wrap each loaf loosely in microwave wrap. Place all loaves in a plastic container. Refrigerate or freeze.

(Metric equivalents: 1 cup = 235 ml, 1 tsp. = 5 ml)

CREATIVE IDEAS TO REFRESH YOUR LITURGICAL PLANNING!

USING ART IN SUNDAY WORSHIP

Eileen Gurak

Paperbound, $7.95
80 pages, 5 1/2" x 8 1/2"
ISBN: 0-89390-186-5
This little book takes the principles found in *Environment and Art in Catholic Worship* and *The General Instruction of the Roman Missal* and applies them to Sunday worship. The author distinguishes between religious and liturgical art — and shows how even newcomers can decorate appropriately and organize your worship space for maximum participation. Helpful illustrations.

THE MODERN LITURGY PLANNING GUIDE

Robert Zappulla, et al.

Paperbound, $19.95
438 pages, 6" x 9"
ISBN 0-89390- 088-5
A great planning resource for liturgists! You'll receive a Scripture commentary, idea starters, and music suggestions for every Sunday of Cycles A, B, and C of the Roman lectionary— along with seasonal comments and suggestions in a workbook format so that you can retain your notes for the next cycle.

SYMBOLS FOR ALL SEASONS:
Planning Worship Environments for Cycles A, B, and C

Catherine H. Krier

Paperbound, $9.95
175 pages, 5 1/2" x 8 1/2"
ISBN 0-89390-125-3
Chock-full of environment ideas and descriptions of symbols based on the Sunday lectionary readings of all three cycles, this book also gives you tips on liturgy planning, artistic considerations, and color. Includes space to jot down your own ideas.

IT'S A BANNER YEAR!

George Collopy

Paperbound, $11.95
211 perforated pages, 6" x 9"
ISBN: 0-89390-176-8
If you're looking for fresh banner ideas or fresh ways to hang them, you'll love these patterns from the award-winning art director of *Modern Liturgy* magazine. More than 100 banner and temporary-art designs for liturgical seasons, sacraments, and secular holidays. Designs have grid overlays for easy reproduction.

PARISH MINISTRY RESOURCES

PREPARING CHILDREN FOR LITURGY:
A Catechist's Guide
Armandine Kelly
Paperbound, $4.95
140 pages, 4 1/4" x 5 7/8"
ISBN O-089390-155-5
This booklet shows catechists how to set the stage so that children can have successful worship experiences. Part one shows you how to activate children's senses. Part two shows you how to help children understand specific parts of the Mass. Part three shows how liturgy is connected to life.

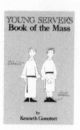

THE YOUNG SERVER'S BOOK OF THE MASS
Kenneth Guentert
Paperbound, $4.95
(Bulk prices available)
73 pages, 4" x 6"
ISBN 0-89390-078-8
This book teaches servers the history of the Mass, which explains to them why they do what they do. You'll be pleased with the results: they'll feel and act like a special part of the liturgy.

LECTOR BECOMES PROCLAIMER
Original edition.
Jerry DuCharme and Gail DuCharme
Paperbound, $4.95
(Bulk prices available)
74 pages, 4" x 6"
ISBN 0-89390-059-1
Train your lectors with this handy booklet. The authors explore the ministry and spirituality of proclamation, provide basic hints for good proclamation, and provide a prayerful method for preparing to proclaim Scripture.

ORDER FORM

Order from your local religious bookstore, or mail this form to:

Qty	Title	Price	Total

Subtotal _____
California Residents Add 6¼% Sales Tax _____
*Postage and Handling _____
Total Amount Enclosed _____

*Postage and Handling:
$1.50 for orders under $10.00
$2.00 for orders of $10.00-$25.00
9% (max. $7.00) of order for orders over $25.00

RESOURCE Resource Publications, Inc.
160 E. Virginia St., #290
San Jose, CA 95112
408 286-8505 FAX 408 287-8748

☐ My check or purchase order is enclosed.
☐ Charge my: ☐Visa ☐MC Exp. Date _____
Card # _____-_____-_____-_____

Signature: _____
Name: _____
Institution: _____
Street: _____
City: _____ St ____ Zip _____
Code: **EB**